THE
TAO OF
ELVIS

DAVID H. ROSEN, M.D.

THE TAO OF ELVIS

A HARVEST ORIGINAL

HARCOURT, INC.

SAN DIEGO   NEW YORK   LONDON

Requests for permission to make copies of any part of the work should
be mailed to the following address: Permissions Department, Harcourt, Inc.,
6277 Sea Harbor Drive, Orlando, Florida 32887-6777.

www.HarcourtBooks.com

Elvis Presley Enterprises, Inc. does not substantiate, validate,
or otherwise endorse the contents of this publication.

Library of Congress Cataloging-in-Publication Data
Rosen, David.
The Tao of Elvis/David Rosen.
p.   cm.
ISBN 0-15-600737-1
1. Laozi. Dao de jing.   2. Presley, Elvis, 1935–1977.   I. Title.
BL1900.L35   R66   2002
299'.514—dc21   2001007545

Text set in Futura Book
Designed by Linda Lockowitz

Printed in the United States of America

First Harvest edition 2002
A C E G I K J H F D B

Permissions acknowledgments begin on page 199
and constitute a continuation of the copyright page.

For Rachel
and her
Song of Songs

Tao is forever, and he that possesses it,
though his body ceases, is not destroyed.
DENG MING-DAO

CONTENTS

PREFACE

Elvis Presley is the greatest cultural force
in the twentieth century. He changed everything—music,
language, clothes; it's a whole new social revolution.
LEONARD BERNSTEIN

I love Elvis and hope to see him in heaven.
There'll never be another like that soul brother.
JAMES BROWN

The Tao is the divine principle of Taoism, the oldest Chinese religion, dating from the sixth century B.C. Lao Tzu was the original Taoist master and the author of the *Tao Te Ching*. This book of wisdom, about the art of living, is the main sacred text of Taoism. The Tao, a mysterious force thought to be everywhere, has been called the Way, God, Eternity, Ultimate Meaning, Primal Spirit, Unity, and Spiritual Wholeness.

The Tao is concerned with soul, acceptance, humility, healing, nonviolence, compassion, and balancing opposites, such as good and evil, and the qualities of *yin* (feminine, dark, and receptive) and *yang* (masculine, light, and active). The Tao also interprets the evolution of the psyche or what Carl Jung called "archetypes and the collective unconscious," that is, our archetypal, mythical, and spiritual heritage. The Tao and archetypes are linked. Archetypes (or ancient imprints) are innate predispositions to opposites such as yin and yang, persona and shadow, the great and terrible mother, and the benevolent and malevolent king. Taoism concerns confronting, containing, transcending, and transforming opposites—the task of all individuals, including Elvis.

Elvis Presley represents a modern archetypal king figure who links the individual to our ancient past, to our current society, and to the future through his music and life. He had a numinous or spiritual quality that was expressed through his dramatic image and movement but most importantly through his soulful songs, which are manifestations of the Tao working through him.

The Tao paradoxically means standing still and moving at the same time. *The Tao of Elvis* both grounds Elvis and recognizes that he will always be on the move. As Lao Tzu said, "This is the profound, simple truth: You are the master of your life and death. What you do is what you are." Elvis had the wisdom to know that he was his own master and had the ability to realize his unique potential. His very name means "the force of God" in Hebrew, and his middle name, Aaron, was the name of Moses's brother, a high priest of Israel.

Elvis was a man of Tao who struggled to balance the opposites: poverty and wealth, female and male, old and new, good and evil, king and non-king, joy and sorrow, water and fire, dark and light, and stillness and movement. He embodied the essential elements of Tao that the small child has:

> Free from care, unaware of self,
> He acts without reflection,
> Stays where he is put, does not know why,
> Does not figure things out,
> Just goes along with them,
> Is part of the current.

Elvis was Taoist in the same way that Taoist Master Kwan Saihung considered Casanova to be "the perfect Taoist." Taoist sage and author Deng Ming-Dao, mystified by Kwan Saihung's viewpoint, replied, "Are you sure? He seemed to be a self-indulgent seducer." Kwan Saihung remained strongly affirmative, responding, "But he had insight. He perceived his own nature and did not hesitate to fulfill his destiny. That's why I call him a perfect Taoist."

By the time Elvis was twenty-one (the midpoint of his life) he had lived out the American dream. Yet, Elvis did much more. He foreshadowed the sexual revolution and women's liberation, and as a nonconformist and revolutionary, of sorts, Elvis's style of civil disobedience broke down racial barriers in the music world, which prefigured the civil rights movement. Elvis Presley and Martin Luther King Jr., who both died in Memphis, were folk royalty—agents of cultural change standing for integration and love.

For all of his heroic feats Elvis was crowned king, and the seeds of a mythic Elvis were sown. Alice Walker wrote in her novel *The Temple of My Familiar,* "In Elvis white Americans found a reason to express their longing and appreciation for the repressed Native American and black parts of themselves." When Elvis's Scotch-Irish and Jewish heritage is considered, we see just what a multicultural icon he really is.

The discrepancy between Elvis's true self and false (king) self caused him immense pain and agony. He became extremely despondent and sought refuge through drug usage. Nevertheless, Elvis was on a spiritual quest, which is surely related to his later being seen as a religious figure. His favorite songs were gospels, and central to his spiritual life were the books *The Prophet, The Impersonal Life, Autobiography of a Yogi,* and the *Holy Bible.* He also practiced meditation and belonged to a worldwide yoga organization, the Self-Realization Fellowship.

The Tao was and is operating through America's king. Like the Tao, Elvis is everywhere. Following his death, on August 16, 1977, Elvis became even more popular, evolving into a global mythic figure. Along with Jesus's and Muhammad Ali's, Elvis's image is one of the most widely recognized on Earth. What does this say about him and us? What does it mean that churches have sprung up in Elvis's name? Graceland has become a mecca that draws nearly a million pilgrims a year. Today thousands of impersonators (disciples) spread his word and image around the world. "Sightings" are almost a daily occurrence, while his actual image dominates our cultural landscape. In 1998, twenty-one years after his death, a twenty-four-foot image of Elvis projected on a screen and accompanied by his music sold out Radio City Music Hall. America's king has become such a force that it seems as if history might someday record time as before and after Elvis. Perhaps this is what John Lennon meant when he said, "Before Elvis there was nothing."

America lacks an actual king and queen mythologically linking the people with the divine. The United States also lacks unified spiritual leadership, so we project this deep archetypal need onto our heroes and heroines, particularly rock and movie stars and occasionally presidents such as John F. Kennedy. The undisputed king and queen of this realm are Elvis Presley and Marilyn Monroe (both of whom self-destructed). It seems that Elvis, with his slogan TCB (taking care of business), is a truer symbol of America than Marilyn Monroe. We need Elvis, as on the Elvis postage stamp, to be resurrected as his young true self—just as Elvis needed and searched for the healing spiritual path to transcend and unite his inner split. This may, in part, be the basis for all interest in Elvis—a symbolic expression of the fact that we need to heal our racially and economically divided country and world as well as reintegrate ourselves. Elvis, like a giant mirror, reflects our own struggles with forces of good and evil, and creation and destruction.

In a real way, when we see Elvis we see ourselves. Symbolizing the battle between the true and false selves in us all, Elvis's huge appeal lies in his power as an archetype—his epic rise and fall captures what is in all of us. Through understanding the Tao of Elvis, we can come to better understand ourselves.

The Tao of Elvis is a psychological and philosophical work in that it is about the phenomenon and the experience of Elvis as well as his (and our) pursuit of purpose, spirituality, and wisdom. Following the introduction are forty-two sections on Taoist concepts, one for each year of Elvis's life. It is both chronological and archetypal, as the Tao was and is expressed in Elvis, and in each of us, from birth until death. It also creates a circle as, ideally, Elvis and we in the end regain some of the innocence of childhood.

Elvis's journey is Taoist. It reflects a profound change in our psyches as well as our culture. We can celebrate and delight in Elvis's soulful music and giving nature, and we can empathize with the pain surrounding his losses and his dependence on prescription drugs. However, the ultimate challenge is to look into the Elvis mirror and see his pain as our own pain. Even though Elvis ultimately failed, our goal ought to be to transcend the opposites, undergo a creative transformation, and heal our own souls in the process.

As a boy I listened to the first recordings of Elvis. Late at night I'd play his records in my bedroom and get lost in songs like "That's All Right [Mama]," "Blue Moon of Kentucky," "Good Rockin' Tonight," and "You're a Heartbreaker." I was drawn to the soul in his voice. At the age of eleven I was awestruck when I heard the eerie and astonishing "Heartbreak Hotel." In 1956 I saw Elvis perform in my hometown of Springfield, Missouri, at The Shrine Mosque Auditorium. I was overwhelmed by the way he sang and moved. He was primitive, pulsating with rhythm and blues, but at the same time pure and spiritual. It was as if a genie had been released from the conservative, segregated, conformist bottle of 1950s culture.

What was it about Elvis, his singing, and his movements that drew me and countless others to him? In the seventh-grade talent show, I even donned felt sideburns and did my own version of "Hound Dog." A generation of young people identified with Elvis and his free spirit, including Paul McCartney, who said, "When we were kids, growing up in Liverpool, all we ever wanted to be was Elvis Presley."

In 1975, while doing research in the remote British Shetland Islands, I dreamed of Elvis: I approached him on a Memphis street corner, introduced myself, and asked if he was really Elvis Presley. He answered, "Yes." I then asked him if he would come home with me. Again he said yes. The scene then shifted to my childhood home in Springfield. I introduced Elvis to my family members—the last person was my mother. She said, "I wish I could have been as talented as you are." Elvis said, "Why, thank ya, ma'am." So more than a quarter century ago, the seed was planted for me to take Elvis home.

Thirty-three years after my boyhood infatuation with Elvis, in 1989, I went to Memphis for a conference related to my training to become a Jungian psychoanalyst. At this meeting I failed a crucial exam, and I was feeling terribly dejected. Like innumerable pilgrims, I was drawn to Graceland. After going through the main house, I walked outside, by the old swing set of Elvis's only child, Lisa Marie, and gazed at the back pasture, where Elvis's horses still grazed. Then I went into the Meditation Garden, where something very unexpected happened. There I was—a grown man in a moment of deep silence—suddenly weeping unashamedly in front of the grave of Elvis Presley. I had no idea why I was crying, but at that moment, I decided to write this book. Twelve years later this volume was completed in Pecos, New Mexico, at the St. Frances Hermitage in the Abbey of Our Lady of Guadalupe. It seems fitting for Elvis to be reborn at a monastery since, as the reader will learn, he wanted to be in one.

INTRODUCTION

All I ever wanted was to help people;
love them, lift them up, spread some joy.
ELVIS PRESLEY

Elvis Presley's death deprives our country
of a part of itself. He was unique, irreplaceable.
PRESIDENT JIMMY CARTER

In 1977 President Jimmy Carter called Elvis "a symbol of the country's vitality, rebelliousness, and good humor." While this was true, there is something more—something hallowed—about the soul and spirit of Elvis. Lao Tzu captures it when he says, "Encouraging others, giving freely to all, awakening and purifying the world with each movement and action, you'll ascend to the divine realm in broad daylight." This is what myths are made of. Rock critic Dave Marsh said, "Elvis Presley was more than anything a spiritual leader of our generation." And Bob Dylan maintained, "When I first heard Elvis's voice I just knew that I wasn't going to work for anybody; and nobody was going to be my boss. He is the deity supreme of rock-and-roll religion as it exists in today's form. Hearing him for the first time was like busting out of jail."

The rise and fall of Elvis reflects what has happened or can happen to each and every one of us. We all have a choice. We can follow a healing path of "egocide and transformation." Or we can choose a self-destructive path, as Elvis did, which ended his life prematurely. Elvis might have had "taking care of business" as his motto, but he wasn't able to take care of himself. His family and the Memphis Mafia, Elvis's entourage, were also not able to do so. Why wasn't his maxim "taking care of Elvis"? Had Elvis become such big business that the human being got lost in the whole venture? And what does this mean to us?

Shakespeare said, "The king is but a man." Elvis, too, knew that he was but a man. J. D. Sumner, lead singer of the gospel singing group J. D. Sumner and the Stamps and one of Elvis's idols during his youth, joined Elvis in January of 1972 for Elvis's new season at the International Hotel in Las Vegas. Sumner recounted a moment that took place during a concert that suggests Elvis knew his limitations:

> A woman ran down to the front of the stage, and Elvis leaned forward like he usually did to kiss her. As he did so, he noticed that she was carrying a crown on a small pillow.
>
> "What's that?" he asked her.
>
> "It's for you," she said breathlessly. "You're the King."
>
> Elvis smiled and took her hand. "No, honey," he said, "I'm not the King. Christ is the King. I'm just a singer."

Even though Elvis knew he wasn't a king, he seemed unable to shed the regal status that his fans projected onto him. What prevented Elvis from sacrificing the archetypal king image? Identified with this false king self, Elvis was simply unable to be his true self. So behind the glittering persona of the benevolent king lurked the shadow of a malevolent king.

Elvis represented both the best and worst of the American dream. Music critic Bill Holdship touched on this when he said, "Elvis is loved, he is hated. He was a genius, a fraud. A saint, the devil. The king, the clown. Even more than when he was alive, Elvis has come to symbolize everything great and everything hideous about America."

Elvis may have been aware of his dual identity, when he was first becoming famous. In 1956, after several successful national TV appearances and many hit songs including his first gold record for "Heartbreak Hotel," Elvis was criticized as being vulgar, inciting riots, and contributing to the moral decay of America. But what others saw as immoral, Elvis saw as merely different. He felt he was expressing not raw sexuality, but something akin to spirituality. Elvis didn't like his negative publicity, yet he was Taoist about it, saying, "There ain't nothing I can do about it so I have to accept it, like I accept the good with the bad, the bad with the good."

People everywhere struggle with the same thing that Elvis struggled with: the conflict between good and evil, and their true and false selves. Our only salvation is to transcend and transform the divided warring factions within ourselves. Elvis lost the human battle, but his life and death can provide us with wisdom and a deeper understanding of ourselves. In order to be our true selves, we need to let go of and transform our false selves. We need to shed inauthentic personas and acknowledge our creative genuine selves as well as our own inner, spiritual natures.

The archetypal Elvis serves a useful purpose in reminding us that the sacrifice of our false selves can lead to symbolic deaths and the rebirths of our true selves. Elvis symbolizes an American, and world, myth gone amuck.

The point is not to worship, imitate, or impersonate Elvis and his *false king self,* but rather to recognize and celebrate the spirit of his *true creative self* and therefore discover our *own true selves.* As Lao Tzu said, "Don't go crazy with the worship of idols [or] images...; this is like a new head on top of the head you already have."

How could the early or young Elvis, a quiet—even shy—gentle, kind, polite, innocent, sensitive, and responsible young man, end up so edgy, loud, aggressive, explosive, unkind at times, guilt ridden, depressed, self-destructive, and sometimes insensitive and irresponsible? It is the human condition—to be both true and false. But how far can a soul stretch before it snaps?

Elvis seemed superhuman in his endless performances, his charitable nature, taking care of his extended family and friends, recording over a hundred gold and platinum records, making thirty movies, completing military service, being married, having a child, getting divorced, and having countless relationships with women before, during, and after his marriage. Yet, after his mother died, in 1958, he suffered from depression and, following his divorce, in 1973, from worsening melancholy and drug addiction.

Elvis was intensely, even symbiotically connected to his mother. As a perpetual youth, he was also attracted to young women. Yet he always wanted his girlfriends both to mother him and to serve his sexual needs. He seemed, with a few exceptions such as Ann-Margret, to have difficulty seeing a woman as an equal. It was only near the end of his life that Elvis bridged that gap when he said, "Sex [is] not the answer...you've got to have a spiritual connection with the woman."

Like Robert Louis Stevenson's *Dr. Jekyll and Mr. Hyde,* Elvis had a scary split within himself. His fame and fortune cast him as a king, yet gradually his shadow asserted itself and turned him into a power-hungry man with a fascination for guns and an addiction to drugs. During the last five years of his life, Elvis's personal shadow took on a more menacing character. He shot out TV screens and spoke of hiring a hit man to kill the lover of his wife, Priscilla.

The way to mental health is facing one's shadow and healing one's inner split between good and evil. In 1965, when Elvis had a religious experience, he made a great stride in this direction, but he was unable to sustain it. If he could have transformed his false king self into his true self, most likely he would still be living today.

Did Elvis have a classic midlife crisis, which always carries with it danger and opportunity? Or was it time for his physical life to end and for the archetypal Elvis to rise up from his ashes? Assuming he had a midlife crisis, Elvis unfortunately identified more with danger and lived out the myth of Icarus. He achieved fame and fortune so quickly that he had difficulty coping and staying grounded. Sadly, like Icarus, he flew too close to the sun, his waxen wings melted, and he crashed into the sea. Elvis knew that he was not really the king, that his persona and image were transparent, and that his wings would melt. Did he willingly sacrifice himself, or was he a sacrificial dying god—cast in this role by archetypal fate, that is, the Tao—in an arid culture that needed his lifeblood as moisture, to grow and change? Regardless, "King Elvis" tragically died, while reading a book on the shroud of Jesus. Sitting on the American throne, he fell forward, ending his life in a prayerful position on the thick bathroom carpet.

Lao Tzu describes how the human Elvis, who was so extraordinary, became archetypal:

> Superior people can awaken during times of turmoil to lead others out of the mire. But how can the one liberate the many? By first liberating his own being. He does this not by elevating himself, but by lowering himself.... Completely emancipated from his former false life, he discovers his original pure nature, which is the pure nature of the universe.

Elvis is identified with the archetypes of sorrow, suffering, and sacrifice, which are part of the process of becoming sacred. Perhaps his being part Native American and part Jewish predisposed him to a path of sacred suffering. He was on a spiritual quest, and he said the reason he always wore a Star of David, or a *chai*, the Hebrew symbol of life, and a cross was so that he would not be "kept out of heaven on a technicality."

Apparently Elvis didn't find enough meaning in his suffering, but perhaps we can by looking into the Elvis mirror. The task of our own healing journeys is to transform our battling opposites into a sacred whole so that our lives have meaning and ongoing creative purpose. In this way we can be compassionate with ourselves, rejoice in the spirit and soul of Elvis the human being, and allow the archetypal Elvis to flow with the mysterious Tao.

1

TAO

Elvis thought the Tao was another word for God.
LARRY GELLER (Elvis's spiritual adviser)

The Tao does nothing
   yet there is nothing it doesn't do.
                              LAO TZU

Before Heaven and Earth were, it is already there:
so still, so lonely.
Alone it stands and does not change.
It turns in a circle and does not endanger itself.
One may call it "the Mother of the World."
I do not know its name.
I call it Dao [Tao].
I call it "great."
Great: that means "always in motion."
                              LAO TZU

The Master doesn't take sides;
She welcomes both saints and sinners.
                              LAO TZU

It is a movement, a force, a progression to the vast universe
that is so mighty even the gods are subordinate to it. A
human being cannot know the Tao in its entirety, but one can
learn its principles and live in harmony with it. In this way,
one can follow the stream of life and attain immortality.
                              KWAN SAIHUNG

I'm a soul, a spirit, a force. I have no interest in anything of this world. I want to live in another dimension entirely.

ELVIS PRESLEY

You know, one of the most important things to learn in life is to be able to cope with not having anything to do.

ELVIS PRESLEY

Elvis could be as quiet and reflective as a monk. Within the confines of his isolated life, he remained a deeply spiritual man.

RICK STANLEY (Elvis's stepbrother)

Elvis was both saint and sinner. He was an enigma.

RICK STANLEY

Lao Tzu described the Tao as a "Mystery of mysteries." Elvis, too, could be viewed as an enigma of enigmas. Elvis was and remains a mysterious dark force, considered both king and fool as well as saint and sinner. Yet his life was a very spiritual quest. While in the Arizona desert in 1965, Elvis saw the face of Stalin in a cloud turn into that of Jesus. Almost immediately Jesus and his numinous energy entered Elvis's body. After this religious experience, Elvis went through a death-rebirth experience and said, "I know now. I've got to do something real with my life. I want out. I want to become a monk and join a monastery. I want to be with God now." According to the religious scholar Friedrich Heiler, "A monk should be an angel on earth living in constant remembrance...of the divine Majesty." Elvis seemed to know "the great Tao, that our true essential nature is the 'primal spirit' in which nature and all life are one."

2

OPPOSITES

Elvis's music and his personality, fusing styles of
white country and black rhythm and blues, permanently
changed the face of American popular culture.
<small>PRESIDENT JIMMY CARTER</small>

Know the male,
yet keep to the female:
receive the world in your arms.
                              LAO TZU

The Tao doesn't take sides;
it gives birth to both good and evil.
                              LAO TZU

Know the white,
yet keep to the black:
be a pattern for the world.
If you are a pattern for the world,
the Tao will be strong inside you
and there will be nothing you can't do.
                              LAO TZU

The bright Way seems dim.
The forward Way seems backward.
The level Way seems bumpy.
Plain truth seems sullied.
The great square has no corners.
The great vessel is never completed.
The great note sounds muted.
The great image has no form.
                              LAO TZU

You accept the bad along with the good.

ELVIS PRESLEY

Elvis would bounce back between being incredibly insecure and amazingly confident. And between being selfish and magnanimous.

MARTY LACKER (Member of Elvis's entourage)

It's not black, it's not white. It's not pop, it's not country.

SAM PHILLIPS (Owner of Sun Records,
commenting on "That's All Right [Mama]," Elvis's first hit)

Elvis has a kindred spirit, someone who shared a secret with me—almost a subversive attraction not just to black music but to black culture, to an inchoate striving, a belief in the equality of man.... He was one of the most introspective human beings I've ever met. He wasn't prejudiced. He didn't draw any lines.

SAM PHILLIPS

Elvis was an integrator of opposites, hence always striving for wholeness. He preferred the yin (dark and female) over the yang (light and male), but he encompassed both. Elvis was an amalgam of good and evil. As his stepbrother Rick Stanley said, "The bottom line is that Elvis was predictably spontaneous—a total contradiction." Most likely Elvis would have agreed with the existentialist philosopher Martin Buber, who said, "Contradiction is given me to endure along with my life and also to fulfill; this endurance and fulfillment of the contradiction is the only meaning accessible to me."

3

CHILD

The great man does not lose his child-heart.
MENCIUS (Famous teacher of Confucianism)

He who is in harmony with the Tao
is like a newborn child.
He is never disappointed;
thus his spirit never grows old.

LAO TZU

Can you make your strength unitary
and achieve that softness
that makes you like a little child?

LAO TZU

My bond with the child
[is] the bond of Tao.

CHUANG TZU

Don't lose your ancient virtue
Not losing your ancient virtue
Be a newborn child again.

LAO TZU

From the time I was a kid, I knew something was going to happen to me. I didn't know exactly what, but it was a feeling that the future looked kinda bright.

ELVIS PRESLEY

Elvis grew up a loved and precious child.

PETER GURALNICK (Author of *Last Train to Memphis*)

My total image of Elvis was as a child....He was like a mirror in a way: whatever you were looking for, you were going to find in him....He had all the intricacy of the very simple.

MARION KEISKER (Sam Phillips's partner at Sun Records in Memphis)

Elvis was always a little boy at heart.

RICK STANLEY

Elvis always had a boyish charm, an innocence, and the simple spiritual characteristics of a child. As the Taoist scholar Wu Ch'eng said, "Those who possess the Way are like children. They age without growing old." During the last five years of Elvis's life, his girlfriend Linda Thompson, as well as Elvis's cousin Billy Smith and Billy's wife, Jo, cared for Elvis as "a small child," and they often spoke "baby talk to him."

4

MOTHER

People are born when they receive breath.
Breath is their mother. And spirit dwells in their breath.
When children care for their mother, their breaths
become one and their spirits become still.
TUNG SSU-CHING (Taoist master)

Who knows the mother
understands the child
Who understands the child
keeps the mother safe.

Lao Tzu

I have the heart of a fool: so confused, so dark.
I alone am different from all men:
But I consider it worthy
to seek nourishment from the Mother.

Lao Tzu

The female is the mother.
All creatures revere their mother.

Ts'ao Tao-ch'ung (Taoist nun)

Children are no different
from their mother.
Li Hsi-chai (Taoist master)

I love you so much. I lived my whole life for you. Oh, God, everything I have is gone.

ELVIS PRESLEY (Words wailed at his mother's burial)

Losing my mother was like losing a best friend, a companion, someone to talk to.

ELVIS PRESLEY

He was a mama's boy.

BARBARA PITTMAN (Singer with Sun Records)

Elvis was not a "mama's boy." Nothing could have been further from the truth. He was a loving, devoted son, trying to make up for the hardships his parents had suffered in their lives.

JUNE JUANICO (An early love of Elvis)

Elvis had a special bond with his mother. When his mother died, Elvis's cousin Billy Smith said, "He was white as a sheet. He started to sob this kind of unearthly sound." Later his step-brother, Rick Stanley, said: "Elvis never really got over his mother's death." Nearly all the women in his life, but particularly Priscilla, Linda Thompson, and Ginger Alden, his last girlfriend, had to mother him as well as be his lover. Five months before he died, Elvis dreamed that Ginger turned into his mother. In his dream his mother mounts Sun, one of Elvis's horses, bareback and says, "Son, our love is eternal, I'll never do anything to hurt you, you know that, never. No matter what, our love for each other is unconditional." As she rides off she becomes Ginger again, and she and Sun fly into the sky and clouds, and all Elvis hears is "I'll never leave, I'll never leave you."

5

FATHER

And how shall you rise beyond your days and nights
unless you break the chains which you at the dawn of your
understanding have fastened around your noon hour?
KAHLIL GIBRAN

No one understands a child better
than its father.

    KUAN-TZU (Taoist prime minister)

When a hideous man becomes a father
And a son is born to him
In the middle of the night
He trembles and lights a lamp
And runs to look in anguish
On that child's face
To see whom he resembles.

                    CHUANG TZU

The wise look at the patterns [of father],
but do not feel confined by them.

                    DENG MING-DAO

When people are simple and their lives are good,
they fear authority.

                WANG P'ANG (Taoist scholar)

I made my father retire. There isn't much sense in him working, because I can make more in a day than he can make in a year.

ELVIS PRESLEY (At age twenty-one, in 1956)

Elvis loved his father. The problem was Vernon, not Elvis. Early on, Vernon was basically jealous of Elvis. As the years went by, the normal father-son roles reversed. Elvis became the provider.

MARTY LACKER

The Colonel is almost like a daddy to me when I'm away from home.

ELVIS PRESLEY

I picked up on Elvis's attitude toward Vernon. I didn't particularly care for him either. I thought he was pretty selfish and just along for the ride. I don't think he was any kind of a father for Elvis. There seemed to be a big vacuum there.

ANN FINCH (Friend of Elvis's, 1960–62)

While Elvis loved his father, he harbored ambivalent feelings toward him. When Elvis was just three, Vernon was imprisoned for forgery. Elvis never overcame a feeling of abandonment. This feeling had set up a negative father complex that was later projected onto his manager, Colonel Tom Parker, who was neither a real colonel nor a good father figure. Despite being a shady character who took up to half (and probably more) of Elvis's earnings, the Colonel propelled Elvis from being a successful regional singer to a national and international superstar. In a noteworthy reflection, Jung maintained that in men, having a positive relationship with their fathers "very often produces a certain credibility with regard to authority and a distinct willingness to bow down before all spiritual dogmas and values." This may be, in part, why Elvis was such a rebel and on his own, unique spiritual quest.

6

FAMILY AND FRIENDS

Family and friends: mysterious cement of the soul.
ROBERT BLAIR (English poet)

Honor your parents,
love your children,
help your brothers and sisters,
be faithful to your friends,
care for your mate with devotion.

LAO TZU

The first practice in the practice of undiscriminating virtue:
take care of those who are deserving; also, and equally,
take care of those who are not.

LAO TZU

We cannot be friends without trust.

DENG MING-DAO

When you think of others before yourself,
that is Tao.

DENG MING-DAO

I was raised in a pretty decent home and everything. My folks always made me behave whether I wanted to or not. I've always had a kind of a common life, we never had any luxuries but we were never real hungry, you know. Now my folks are just real proud, just like I am.

ELVIS PRESLEY

Elvis treated me better and with more respect than anyone else I had ever met. He would take the time. He would listen intently.... Anything I would ask for, he'd give it to me.

MACK GURLEY (Longstanding friend,
who picked up Elvis hitchhiking in 1950)

Elvis was an enormously loving parent.... Elvis gave [Lisa Marie]... unequivocal love.... He had no hesitation, no qualms about saying, "Your daddy loves you so much," and he would get tears in his eyes telling her. He would laugh with her. He was very physically demonstrative in his affection, which is also very important. She knew that her daddy adored her.

LINDA THOMPSON (Elvis's steady girlfriend, 1972–1976)

We were all together so much; we were all very much influenced by Elvis, because, let's face it, he was the center of everything that went on.... It was family, we all had our one-on-one relationships with Elvis, and everybody thought that was *the* special relationship. Elvis had a spiritual charisma about him that made you feel like he was your best friend, and you could always depend on him.

JERRY SCHILLING (Member of the Memphis Mafia,
speaking about Elvis and his entourage)

Elvis was very trusting, and based on the work of the developmental psychologist Erik Erikson, trust develops in the first two years of life when there is a good mother-infant bond. Erikson links trust to hope and faith as well as to being true and loyal with family and friends. Elvis loved and revered his parents, daughter, extended family, entourage, and many friends (girlfriends and ex-wife included). Elvis's positive relationship with his mother, according to Jung, gave him "a great capacity for friendship, which often creates ties of astonishing tenderness between men and may even rescue friendships between the sexes from the limbo of the impossible."

7

SPIRIT, SOUL, AND RELIGION

You have walked among us as a spirit.
KAHLIL GIBRAN

The world is a spiritual thing.
LAO TZU

Can you educate your soul
so that it encompasses the One?
LAO TZU

To arrive at the unshakable, you must befriend the Tao....
Simply see that you are at the center of the universe, and
accept all things and beings as parts of your infinite body.
LAO TZU

Everything we do is Tao.
Spirituality is...all around us and in us.
DENG MING-DAO

I always knew there was a truth to my religion. Somehow I never lost faith in God.

Elvis Presley

Elvis was pure soul—pure soul, an astute human being.

Larry Geller

Elvis is becoming a religion unto himself.... The Church of the Risen Elvis... and... The First Presleyterian Church...They might as well just build the Graceland convent.

Lamar Fike (Member of Elvis's entourage)

The Gospel of Elvis is meant to teach the religion of Elvis: Elvis-ism...God split the Othermind into two (the goddess of sleep, to draw man into dark slumber, and the god of wakefulness, to excite man into light and action), similar to Lao Tzu's Taoist creation story of the universe splitting into the first duality, *yin* and *yang*.

Louie Ludwig (Author of *The Gospel of Elvis*)

Elvis's close bond with his mother may have predisposed him to spirit, soul, and religion. As Elvis's friend Ann Finch said:

> "Elvis often spoke of his mother with great love and affection. He was very spiritual and expressed it through music. Elvis preferred gospel music, as did his mother. Often our time together was spent with Elvis at the piano singing gospel songs."

In commenting on the effects of a man's strong relationship with his mother, Jung said, "Often he is endowed with a wealth of religious feelings, which help to bring the *ecclesia spiritualis* into reality; and a spiritual receptivity, which makes him responsive to revelation." Clearly Elvis's spirit and soul were connected to his mother and their love of gospel music.

8

LOVE

Much have we loved you....
And ever has it been
that love knows not its own depth
until the hour of separation.
KAHLIL GIBRAN

Through love one may be courageous.
LAO TZU

Kindness in giving creates love.
LAO TZU

Love your life.
Trust the Tao.
Make love with the invisible subtle origin of the universe,
and you will give yourself everything you need.
LAO TZU

The deeper the love
The higher the cost.
LAO TZU

My moment of glory is being on that stage and singing and feeling all the love the audience sends to me. It's a completed circle of love we send each other. It's beyond any mortal high.

ELVIS PRESLEY

Elvis was sweet. I don't know what it was about that boy, but you could just love him to death.

CHRISTINE ROBERTS PRESLEY (Great aunt)

Elvis had a great capacity for love.

LINDA THOMPSON

Everyone knew Elvis wasn't perfect, but they loved him for his music and for who he was. I loved him for the love he had given me.

RICK STANLEY

Elvis's love was expressed often and in profound and focused ways. He deeply loved his mother, Gladys, whose middle name was Love. Elvis loved many women; they loved him in return, and for quite a number, the love was everlasting.

Of course, his wife, Priscilla, gave birth to the major love of his life. Elvis said, "My love for Lisa Marie comes first: she's number one."

Of his special love relationship with his audience Elvis said, "It's like a surge of electricity going through you. It's almost like making love, but it's even stronger than that...Sometimes I think my heart is going to explode."

Although he loved intensely and passionately, tragically he was not able to ward off love's twin, "strife," best described by Kahlil Gibran, "For even as love crowns you so shall he crucify you."

America, with its excessive divorce rate, also has a problem with love, often confusing it with sexuality and allowing strife to flourish. While eros is important, philos, or friendship, is the bridge to agape, a deep spiritual love. This quote from Henry David Thoreau captures what happened to America's king and how Elvis still lives:

All that a man has to say or do that can possibly concern mankind is, in some shape or other, to tell the story of his love—and to sing; and if he is fortunate and keeps alive, he will be forever in love.

9

MUSIC AND SONG

Music is the mediator between
the spiritual and the sensual life.
BEETHOVEN

A good artist lets his intuition
lead him wherever it wants.

LAO TZU

Hold up the Great Image
and the world will come
and be beyond harm
safe serene and at one
fine food and song
detain passing guests
when the Tao speaks.

LAO TZU

Performed with the harmony of yin and yang,
Illuminated with the brightness of the sun and moon.
Performed with notes that would not weary
And that were turned to a scale of spontaneity.
[The music] fills heaven and earth to the brim
It envelops the six poles of the universe.

CHUANG TZU

When the center is genuine
and that is reflected in the emotions,
there is music.

CHUANG TZU

My voice is God's will, not mine.

ELVIS PRESLEY

Elvis sang songs that were popular and a lot of the old blues-type songs; he did some of the old spirituals, too. Right from the start it was as if he had a power over people, it was like they were transformed.

DIXIE LOCKE (Elvis's girlfriend, 1954)

He was really a natural. When Elvis was performing, everyone had the same basic reaction. It was almost spontaneous...seeing these people get religion.

TOM PERRYMAN (Promoter and booking agent,
regarding Elvis's early performances on
the Louisiana Hayride in Shreveport)

There was a floating sense of inner harmony mixed with a ferocious hunger, a desperate striving linked to a pure outpouring of joy, that seemed to just tumble out of the music. It was the very attainment of art and passion, the natural beauty of the instinctive soul.

PETER GURALNICK, Last Train to Memphis
(Commenting on Elvis's recording of "Mystery Train")

Elvis expressed soul in his songs, and he felt that his purpose in life was to give voice to the power of the Lord. So, in a real sense, he knew that he was expressing the Divine Mystery, or Tao. Elvis put it this way, "I feel God and his goodness, and I believe I can express his love for us in music."

Elvis actualized India's inspired Nobel Laureate poet Rabindranath Tagore's sentiment about the bliss of singing: "I forget myself and call Thee friend who art my Lord." Listening to Elvis's rendering of "How Great Thou Art," it is clear that Elvis and Tagore were on the same wavelength.

10

GRACE AND GENTLENESS

Simple grace...gently penetrating.
I Ching

The man [of] Tao
Acts without impediment
Yet he does not know himself
To be kind [and] gentle.
CHUANG TZU

Gentleness (a cardinal virtue) manifests as kindness,
consideration for others, and sensitivity to spiritual truth.
LAO TZU

With gentleness and goodness,
you will win their hearts.
I CHING

Make your mood gentle and your mind comfortable,
then enter into quietude.
TUNG-PIN LÜ (Author of *The Secret of the
Golden Flower: A Chinese Book of Life*)

All good flows through grace.

ELVIS PRESLEY

Elvis was a gentle boy. [One time] I asked him to go hunting with me, but when he answered, "Daddy, I don't want to kill birds," I didn't try to persuade him to go against his feelings.

VERNON PRESLEY

His small child's voice carries a quavering note of yearning—other children get up and do letter-perfect recitals, big burly men frail on their beat-up guitars, but Elvis cradles his like a bird.

PETER GURALNICK, Last Train to Memphis
(Commenting on Elvis performing when he was a child)

Elvis never had formal dance training...but he had that natural rhythm....He couldn't seem to make a mistake; even if it was wrong, it was right.

JANICE PENNINGTON (An Elvis fan who became
a good friend, referring to his dancing in Jailhouse Rock)

When Elvis bought his home, Graceland, he joined spirit (Father Sky) with land (Mother Earth). From the beginning Elvis was a shy and gentle soul. Many considered him a gentleman. He exhibited grace in his movements and in song. Elvis embodied Rabbi Abraham Joshua Heschel's reflection:

> "One feels it a grace to be able to give oneself up to music, to a tone, to a song. The wave of a song carries the soul to heights which utterable meanings can never reach."

Hexagram 14 (of the *I Ching*), having to do with supreme success, seems to capture the Tao of Elvis:

> Possession in great measure is determined by fate and accords with the time, which is favorable—a time of strength within, clarity and culture without. Power is expressing itself in a graceful and controlled way. This brings supreme success and wealth.

11

DARKNESS, SORROW, AND SADNESS

Where there is sorrow, there is holy ground.
OSCAR WILDE

The one we call dark
the dark beyond dark
the door to all beginnings.
LAO TZU

The birth of a man
is the birth of his sorrow.
CHUANG TZU

Inside there is a creature
it's distant and dark
but inside there is an essence
an essence fundamentally real
and inside there is a heart.
LAO TZU

The brightest path seems dark.
LAO TZU

[Elvis was] a sad, shy... boy.

KENNETH HOLDITCH (Childhood classmate)

Elvis always seemed to me to be very, very sad.

ANN FINCH

I've made a study of Marlon Brando,... poor Jimmy Dean,... [and] myself, and I know why girls... go for us. We're sullen, we're broodin', we're something of a menace.

ELVIS PRESLEY

I felt sorry for Elvis, because he didn't enjoy life the way he should. He stayed indoors all the time.

MUHAMMAD ALI
(A lifelong fan, commenting on Elvis's sadness)

Elvis was at times full of sadness and sorrow. He preferred living in dark cavelike rooms. Elvis's bedroom was windowless, and his hotel rooms were sealed so that no light could seep in. In Elvis's darkness, however, he realized many dreams and fulfilled much of his potential. As Taoist scholar Red Pine (Bill Porter) said:

> The Tao, the dark...the essence, the Way; and Te, the light...the spirit, Virtue...The dark gives the light a place to shine. The light allows us to see the dark. But too much light blinds. Lao Tzu saw everyone chasing the light and hastening their own destruction. He encouraged people to choose the dark instead of the light, less instead of more, weakness instead of strength, inaction instead of action. What could be simpler?

Sadly, in the last years of Elvis's life, when he needed light, his drug addiction drowned him in total darkness. Nevertheless, on some deep level Elvis resonated with Lao Tzu's saying:

> The Tao is dark and unfathomable.
> How can it make [him] radiant?
> Because [he] lets it.

Meaningfully, however, Elvis was bathed in a brilliant holy light as the curtain was coming down on his earthly existence.

12

LIGHT, FIRE, AND PASSION

The passions are like fire, useful in a thousand ways
and dangerous only in one, through their excess.
CHRISTIAN BOVEE (American author)

In the deep dark he alone sees light.
CHUANG TZU

The light itself is *the creative*.
TUNG-PIN LÜ

In passion we see the end.
LAO TZU

Where the fountains of passion
Lie deep
The heavenly springs
Are soon dry.
CHUANG TZU

Send me some light—I need it bad.

> ELVIS PRESLEY (He said this prayer
> before performances)

I'm afraid I'll go out like a light, just like I came on.

> ELVIS PRESLEY

He's just a great big, beautiful hunk of forbidden fruit.

> (A female student of Mae Axton's, who was a teacher
> and early promoter of Elvis in Florida)

Music ignited a fiery pent-up passion inside Elvis and inside me. It was an odd, embarrassing, funny, inspiring, and wonderful sensation.

> ANN-MARGRET (Elvis's leading lady
> in the movie *Viva Las Vegas*)

Elvis was passionate—on fire—and a light to many. But his light dimmed after his mother died, and darkness set in following his divorce. Almost prophetically Wang Tao's statement rings true: "Light does not come from light, but from dark." After Elvis made out his will in early March, 1977, he was shaken by a dream in which he saw "The face of God." It manifested itself in the form of "a white light so bright" he almost couldn't look at it.

13

DREAMS

Your youth has given us dreams to dream.
KAHLIL GIBRAN

Life is like a dream, ... so there is no good
in taking it too seriously.

DENG MING-DAO

Dreams are the roaming of the spirit.

TUNG-PIN LÜ

Once upon a time, I, Chuang Tzu, dreamed I was a butterfly
flying happily here and there, enjoying life without knowing
who I was. Suddenly, I woke up and I was indeed Chuang
Tzu. Did Chuang Tzu dream he was a butterfly, or did the
butterfly dream he was Chuang Tzu? There must be some
distinction between Chuang Tzu and the butterfly. This is a
case of transformation.

CHUANG TZU

By and by, there will be a great awakening;
then we will know that this is all a great dream.

CHUANG TZU

My whole life is a dream. I hope I never wake up.

ELVIS PRESLEY

I was running and jumping over tall buildings—like I was Superman or something.

ELVIS PRESLEY (Recounting a dream)

My life's a fairy tale. It's like a dream. And I'm living it.

ELVIS PRESLEY

It's like Elvis came along and whispered a dream in everybody's ear, and then we all dreamed about it somehow.

BRUCE SPRINGSTEEN

Elvis sought meaning in everything; particularly his dreams. A couple of years before he died, Elvis reported an important dream, which Larry Geller recorded:

> Elvis and Lisa Marie are somewhere in the Holy Land following Armageddon. There's destruction everywhere, and they're traveling around in a large armored vehicle, like a tank. Typically, Elvis's armored vehicle is being driven by a chauffeur. Lisa begins crying. Elvis looks at her and says, "Don't worry, honey. Don't worry, honey. Nothing's going to happen to your daddy. There's always going to be an Elvis."
>
> Unlike many of his dreams, this wasn't one Elvis had to ponder long to understand. In his own mind, outside of his very self, there was *another* Elvis.

C. G. Jung said about dreaming that "it shows the inner truth and reality of the person as it really is. Not as he conjectures it to be, and not as he would like it to be, but *as it is*."

Elvis seemed to realize that he would live on as an archetypal Elvis.

14

GIVING AND GENEROSITY

See first that you yourself deserve to be a giver,
and an instrument of giving.
KAHLIL GIBRAN

The more he does for others
The greater his existence
The more he gives to others
The greater his abundance.

LAO TZU

He is humane who has long been generous
with valuable goods to make people happy,
so that they enjoy their lives.

LAO TZU

When first one considers others
besides oneself, spirituality arrives.

DENG MING-DAO

He gives his wealth to the poor and uses his virtue
to teach the unwise. And like
the sun or moon,
he never stops shining.

HO-SHANG KUNG (Taoist master)

I'm so lucky to be in the position to give. It's really a gift to give.

ELVIS PRESLEY

Elvis was always giving someone something.

SONNY WEST (Member of Elvis's entourage)

You're giving when you don't know you're giving.

ELVIS PRESLEY

Elvis was the most generous of men.

LINDA THOMPSON

Elvis's generous and giving nature is well documented. Elvis's dentist and friend, Dr. Lester Hofman, explained, "Elvis had a special way with people, and he was always giving you gifts." Elvis gave Dr. Hofman and his wife, Sterling, his friendship, but also a new car and an organ, both of which they keep in mint condition. Sterling also said that Elvis taught her yoga—she currently leads a yoga group of multiple sclerosis patients—and that he gave her a signed book on yoga, which she keeps in a safety deposit box.

Elvis gave tens of millions of dollars to local and national religious and social charities. On a more personal note, when Jerry Schilling, one of the Memphis Mafia, told Elvis of his interracial marriage to Myrna Smith, of the Sweet Inspirations, Elvis responded with emotional support—and bought them a new home. Elvis had first met Jerry in 1954, as a twelve-year-old filling in for a team that needed an extra player in a touch football game. At the official housewarming, Elvis said, "I know I drove all those other guys [the other members of the Mafia] crazy buying you this house, but your mother died when you were a year old, and you never had a home, and I wanted to be the one to give it to you."

15

ALONE AND LONELINESS

As soon as you are really alone you are with God.
THOMAS MERTON

What men hate is forlornness,
loneliness, being a trifle.
And yet, princes and kings
choose these to describe themselves.

LAO TZU

All spirituality begins and ends with the self.

DENG MING-DAO

Other people are excited,
as though they were at a parade.
I alone don't care.

LAO TZU

To live the life of Tao is a lonely life.

DENG MING-DAO

People think I'm lonely, but I love that lonesome feelin'.

ELVIS PRESLEY

Elvis was a loner. He liked people, but he was quiet.

ELOIS BEDFORD (Elvis's first girlfriend,
second through fifth grades)

I get lonesome right in the middle of a crowd.

ELVIS PRESLEY

Elvis was an intensely lonely person, so alone with his fame and his thoughts.

BILL BROWDER (One of Elvis's friends)

The word *alone* derives from "all One" and can mean being close to God. It's fitting that, being a religious person, Elvis liked to be alone. He was also sad and sometimes lonely. As Elvis once said, "I swear to God, no one knows how lonely I get. And how empty I feel." But it was this very emptiness that allowed Elvis to contact "Spirit." Unable to sustain it, however, Elvis filled the emptiness with drugs, to dull and eventually escape the pain from the fame of his false self. This relates to John Lennon's theory about what killed Elvis: "The king is always killed by his courtiers. He is overfed, overindulged, overdrunk to keep him tied to the throne. Most people in the position never wake up."

16

TWINNING AND PAIRING

Whether laughing or crying all I hear is an echo.
SOEN NAKAGAWA (Zen master)

The coexistence of have and have not
The coproduction of hard and easy
The codependence of high and low
The correspondence of note and noise
The coordination of first and last
is endless.

LAO TZU

So everything we feel of the world is always the Tao of two, or to put it another way, the relative Tao. And the relative, by definition, cannot be the absolute One.

DENG MING-DAO

The existence of things, the difficulty of affairs, the size of forms, the magnitude of power, the pitch and clarity of sound, the sequence of position, all involve contrasting pairs. When one is present, both are present. When one is absent, both are absent.

WU CH'ENG

[Tao] causes being and non-being
But is neither being nor non-being.
CHUANG TZU

They say when one twin dies, the other grows with all the qualities of the other, too. If I did, I'm lucky.

> ELVIS PRESLEY (Referring to the death
> of his twin, Jesse Garon, at birth)

As Elvis's life grew larger and larger...Jesse (his dead twin brother) remained a constant. The shadow that would forever haunt him.

> PETER WHITMER (Author of *The Inner Elvis*)

[At] the funeral when Elvis's uncle died...there sat Elvis and Priscilla, looking like twins! Elvis had blue eyes; Priscilla had blue eyes. Elvis had his hair dyed coal-black; Priscilla had her hair dyed coal-black.

> GERALDINE KYLE (Good friend of
> Elvis's stepmother, Dee Stanley)

I dreamed that you were my twin, and you let me come out first—but while you were saving me by letting me be born first, you suffocated to death.

> ELVIS PRESLEY (In 1975 Elvis told Linda Thompson
> about this dream in which she was his twin, who died)

The loss, at birth, of Jesse Garon, his twin brother, represented something positive (empathy, love, and joy) and negative (ache, emptiness, and sorrow). It resulted in overprotectiveness by his mother, that is, Elvis was paired with her, particularly early on in Elvis's life, when his father was away. This was a kind of twinning that would continue with other women be-fore—and especially after—his mother's death. Carrying the tension of the opposites and evolving to a higher level allows for great creativity. Elvis's songs served this purpose, and when singing, he was able to get it together and be at peace. In Elvis's twinning we can see both integration and disintegra-tion, happiness and unhappiness, as well as success and failure.

17

MAN OF TAO

All those who follow Tao become eccentric.
DENG MING-DAO

The Man of [Tao] disregards himself,
and his Self is increased.
He gives himself away
and his Self is preserved.

Lao Tzu

Thus also is the Man of [Tao]:
he encompasses the One
and sets an example to the world.
He does not want to shine,
therefore will he be enlightened.
He does not want to be anything for himself,
therefore he becomes resplendent.
He does not lay claim to glory,
therefore he accomplishes works.
He does not seek excellence,
therefore he will be exalted.

Lao Tzu

Thus also is the Man of [Tao]:
he sets an example without cutting others down to size;
he is conscientious without being hurtful;
he is genuine without being arbitrary;
he is bright without being blinding.

Lao Tzu

Whoever knows himself is wise.
Whoever conquers himself is strong.
Whoever asserts himself has will-power.
Whoever is self-sufficient is rich.
Whoever does not lose his place [endures].
Whoever does not perish in death lives.

Lao Tzu

Man, all I did is what came natural! I guess if you have a dirty ol' mind, that's exactly what you're gonna see in others.

ELVIS PRESLEY

Elvis was just so different, all the other guys were like replicas of their dads....Inside,...I think he knew he was different. I knew the first time I met him that he was not like other people....He was not a phony, he was not a put-on, he was not a show-off, and once you were around him long enough to see him be himself, not just act the clown, anyone could see his real self, you could see his sweetness, you could see the humility.

DIXIE LOCKE

Elvis came in to make a record one Saturday....Elvis had to wait awhile (there were a lot of people there), but he...was very polite. While I was getting ready, I asked him what kind of singer he was. He told me he sang all kinds of songs. I asked him, "Well, who do you sound like?" He said, "I don't sound like nobody." We got all set up—he had his guitar with him—and he recorded two songs: "That's When Your Heartaches Begin" and "My Happiness" and something struck me about him.

MARION KEISKER

Elvis's love for people was his greatest quality. He tried to help everyone....He could have anything, and he shared it beautifully.

MACK GURLEY

Elvis was a man of Tao: singular, natural, spiritual, kind, and humble. All these traits and more were described by one of Elvis's co-stars in *Wild in the Country*, Millie Perkins, who said:

> "Elvis...was a man...who truly cared about people. He was this very humble person...with a refined heart and soul....The essence of Elvis was as fine a person as I've ever met."

In some way, through the ecstasy and the agony of fame, the profound loss of his mother, the pain of divorce, and the madness of drug addiction, Elvis embodied the Tao. Perhaps Wu Ch'eng was right to ask and answer the basic question that clearly pertained to Elvis: "Lao Tzu extols simplemindedness and weakness over wisdom and strength. Why then does he also extol wisdom and strength? Wisdom and strength are for dealing with the inside. Simplemindedness and weakness are for dealing with the outside."

18

INNOCENCE AND PLAY

Verily the ocean laughs always with the innocent.
KAHLIL GIBRAN

In innocence we see the beginning.

LAO TZU

Innocence is inside us, and we need to go inside to find it. Those who follow Tao emphasize the concept of returning [to it].

DENG MING-DAO

Innocence does not need to make efforts. Innocence does not need to belong to groups. Innocence does not need to be anything. Innocence is inherently pure, and that inherent purity is Tao.

DENG MING-DAO

Playing is as precious as jade and helps us find our way back to the beginning—the source.

DENG MING-DAO

Elvis looked like an innocent little boy.

JUNE JUANICO

Elvis was always real hyper. He would run and play so hard, he'd just wear himself out.

HAROLD LLOYD (Elvis's first cousin)

Elvis didn't radiate purity, yet something about his innocence has always [shone] through. And I believe that is because he was an honest man who sincerely cared about those he loved and about those who loved him.

LARRY GELLER

It didn't matter what he did. He would act silly or say something silly—get the words wrong or make up words. He just couldn't do anything wrong. But it was because…he really loved his audience. He loved his fans more than anybody I've ever seen.

WANDA JACKSON (A singer who traveled with Elvis)

Like the Tao, Elvis loved to move and play with passion. He also, like the Tao, was fond of meditation and stillness. Elvis embodied these wise Taoist words of Ts'ao Tao-ch'ung:

> Innocence and passion, or in other words, stillness and movement...provisionally different, they are ultimately the same.

In the words of Moriz Cammerloher, an expert on art and depth psychology, Elvis had "this [God-given] talent for giving oneself entirely to the free flow of one's thoughts or ideas, feelings or intuitions, this ability to play...[which] is the secret of the creative mind."

19

KNOWLEDGE AND WISDOM

Reading gives God more glory when we
get more out of it, when it is a more deeply vital act
not only of our intelligence but of our whole personality,
absorbed and refreshed in thought, meditation,
prayer, or even in the contemplation of God.
THOMAS MERTON

Mastering books is part of mastery of Tao.
DENG MING-DAO

Knowing others is intelligence;
knowing yourself is true wisdom.
LAO TZU

For he who knows does not speak,
He who speaks does not know.
LAO TZU

Tao is the middle way. We cannot have one side
without the other in life: it is wisdom to strike a balance
between them both.

DENG MING-DAO

A long time ago, someone very special [June Juanico] gave me a book to read [*The Prophet* by Kahlil Gibran]. I've read it at least a million times.... It's my favorite book. I try to keep a copy with me at all times. It's my unwinder. It helps me relax and forget everything.

ELVIS PRESLEY

Although it hardly fits his public image as the King of Rock and Roll, Elvis was a voracious and careful reader. The books we shared offered ideas about religion [and] God.... Almost all of the works dealt with abstract metaphysical concepts, and some were written in an archaic, convoluted style that can be difficult to follow. He impressed me with his diligence and determination to understand each word he read. Before long, you rarely saw Elvis when he wasn't carrying his newest book and a dictionary. [He was] inquisitive by nature and eager to learn.

The first work Elvis read was *The Impersonal Life* by Joseph Benner, [which] appealed to Elvis for several reasons: it speaks of purpose, of an intelligence—God, if you will—guiding seekers to the knowledge of God within us all.

LARRY GELLER

He had incredible native intelligence, the ability to read a human being, to watch someone's eyes and look inside their soul.

BOB ABEL (Filmmaker, along with his partner
Pierre Adidge, of *Elvis on Tour*)

I have my own way of learning. I learn from the people I work with. I learn from everyday life itself.

ELVIS PRESLEY

Elvis craved knowledge, particularly of a spiritual nature. And as the Taoist Loy Ching Yuen said, "Knowledge comes with perseverance." Elvis was on a lifelong quest to figure out why he was picked to be Elvis. He felt that he was chosen by God for a special purpose, and he read widely, seeking spiritual knowledge. As his spiritual adviser, Larry Geller, said, "He remained a Christian his whole life, but... he was open to other beliefs and teachings." Once you experience or live the spiritual knowledge, it becomes wisdom. Angelus Silesius, the Catholic mystic, stated, "Wisdom laughs to be where her children are—why? O Miracle! She herself is a child."

20

IMAGE (PERSONA AND SHADOW)

Your shadow has been a light upon our faces.
KAHLIL GIBRAN

Whoever holds fast to the great primal image,
to him the world will come.
It comes and is not violated:
In calmness, equity and blessedness.
Music and allurement:
They may well make the wanderer stop in his tracks.

LAO TZU

If a man, born in Tao,
Sinks into the deep shadow
Of non-action
To forget aggression and concern,
He lacks nothing
His life is secure.

CHUANG TZU

Image refers to the breath of something before it is born.

WU CH'ENG

The Great Image has no form [it is the Great Way]. To hold means to focus or keep. Those who can keep their body in the realm of Dark Virtue and focus their mind on the gate of Hidden Serenity possess the Way. All things come to them. Clouds appear...rain pours down, and all creatures are refreshed...and...nourished."

LI JUNG (Taoist master)

The image is one thing the human being is another... it's very hard to live up to an image.

ELVIS PRESLEY

They know about Elvis, the image, but not...the inner me.

ELVIS PRESLEY

No one can live up to that image and survive.

ELVIS PRESLEY

The interesting thing about Elvis, unlike most famous people, he looked and moved and spoke exactly as he did on television or in the movies. It struck me that Elvis didn't "develop" an image for public consumption: on some level, he was his image. On the other hand, his low-key manner and friendly demeanor seemed incongruous, as if he were trying to tell you, yes, he was Elvis Presley, but he was someone else, too. Over the years I would come to see how wide a line divided the public Elvis, the man we all thought we knew, from the private Elvis, the man he wanted us all to understand.

LARRY GELLER

When we look at our image in a mirror, it's critical that we see not only our outer persona, but also our shadow and inner soul. Elvis realized that his image was merely a part of himself and that his true self was not visible to others. He told Linda Thompson, "They don't know me. They just look at me. They love what I can do, that I can sing, that I move the way that I do. But they don't know my heart. And they don't know my soul." Once, on the verge of tears, Elvis said to Larry Geller, "Do you realize I'll never know if a woman loves me or Elvis Presley."

The risk of creating and accepting an inflated image and identity is that it can crystallize as a false self. People then treat you as if you are something you are not. And in due course you become something you are not. Since the king archetype exists in everyone, it gets projected onto an unfortunate person cast in the role. This happened to Elvis, and millions of women projected their inner masculine (father, lover, partner, and spiritual figure) onto him. Priscilla Presley did this, as she said, "He taught me everything.... Over the years he became my father, husband, and very nearly God."

21

TRUTH AND TRUTH OF CHARACTER

What is true is real, but nothing more.
SU CH'E (Chinese author)

The truest truth [seems] uncertain.

LAO TZU

In public, we may be pursuing our responsibilities. In our private time, we put all that aside and [attempt] to return to the source. In that returning, we no longer have names, we no longer have anything credited to us. We are who we are, and no more. But who we are at that point: that is truth.

DENG MING-DAO

You have got lost, and are trying
To find your way back
To your own true self.

CHUANG TZU

Those who want to know the truth of the universe should practice the four cardinal virtues:

The first is reverence for all life; this manifests as unconditional love and respect for oneself and all beings.

The second is natural sincerity; this manifests as honesty, simplicity, and faithfulness.

The third is gentleness; this manifests as kindness, consideration for others, and sensitivity to spiritual truth.

The fourth is supportiveness; this manifests as service to others without expectation of reward.

LAO TZU

I knew in my own way. I knew.

ELVIS PRESLEY (Talking about his true calling
to be a singer with a special purpose)

Son,...always remember...no matter what happens when you grow up, never look down on others or think that you are better than they are, because in the eyes of God we are all equal.

GLADYS PRESLEY

There is something magical about watching a man who has lost himself find his way back home.

JOHN LANDAU (Rock critic, in his review of
Elvis's 1968 NBC "Comeback" TV special)

Elvis...was [a]...very loyal person, very loyal friend, very loving man, very funny [human being]; he loved to laugh, loved life, loved living, and loved people.

LINDA THOMPSON

Elvis was true to himself. He embodied the words of Ralph Waldo Emerson; "Insist on yourself; never imitate." In one of Elvis's favorite spiritual books, *The Impersonal Life* by Joseph Benner, Elvis found confirmation of his true self:

> That the truth lies within us all, that God is in fact "the divine I." "Are you ready?"..."Do you *want* to go?... In order that you may learn to know Me, so that you can be sure it is I, your own True Self, who speaks these words, you must first learn to *Be Still*....I may be expressing through you beautiful symphonies of sound...that manifest as music...and which so affects others as to cause them to acclaim you as one of the great ones of the day.

22

HAPPINESS AND JOY

Your joy is your sorrow unmasked....
When you are sorrowful look again in your heart,
and you shall see that in truth you are weeping
for that which has been your delight.
KAHLIL GIBRAN

To increase life is called happiness.
LAO TZU

You never find happiness
until you stop looking for it.
CHUANG TZU

If you practice non-doing (*wu wei*),
you have both happiness and well-being.
CHUANG TZU

Happiness rests on unhappiness;
unhappiness lies in wait for happiness.
LAO TZU

Someone to love, something to look forward to, and something to do.

> ELVIS PRESLEY (Elvis's "Philosophy for a Happy Life"
> written down for his friend, Pat Parry)

Elvis had a great sense of humor—always laughing, telling jokes, and reading to you.

> MYRNA SMITH (Friend and member
> of the Sweet Inspirations)

Elvis was one of the funniest people I ever met...his wry sense of humor and funny way of looking at things had us cracking up most of the time.

> LARRY GELLER

It's...important...to surround yourself with people who can give you a little happiness, because you only pass through this life once...you don't come back for an encore.

> ELVIS PRESLEY

Many believed that Elvis was basically a sad person. Yet Elvis knew laughter and the joy of singing, and he brought happiness to others. We now see that Elvis was Taoist and embodied both sides of art and its creative process. In a poem by Herman Melville these dualities are captured well:

A flame to melt—a wind to freeze;
Sad patience—joyous energies;
Humility—yet pride and scorn.
Instinct and study; love and hate;
Audacity—reverence. These must mate.
And fuse with Jacob's mystic heart,
To wrestle with the angel—Art.

The inner Elvis might have been content to meditate on this verse by Yogananda, whom Elvis loved to read:

From joy I came
For joy I live,
In sacred joy I melt.

23

VIRTUE

The reason people don't understand me
is because my virtue is dark
and not visible from the outside.
HO-SHANG KUNG

The Way begets them
Virtue keeps them.
LAO TZU

Cultivated in the self virtue becomes real.
LAO TZU

He who contains virtue in abundance
resembles a newborn child.
LAO TZU

The virtue of nonaggression
is uniting with Heaven.
LAO TZU

Elvis was good "with a tender heart." That's all I can ever say about him.

LAVERNE FARRAR (Childhood and lifelong friend)

He felt he had been given this gift, this talent, by God. He didn't take it for granted. He thought it was something that he had to protect. He had to be nice to people. Otherwise, God would take it back.

NATALIE WOOD (Actress; dated Elvis during 1956)

Elvis came out for the boxing team at Humes High School. I put him in the ring against Sambo Barrom and this guy bloodied Elvis's nose pretty good. Then Elvis came to me and said, "Coach, I hate to tell you this, but I'm quitting the team. I'm a lover, not a fighter."

WALT DOXEY (High school boxing coach)

I admired Elvis because he was nice to me. . . . I was a younger guy that Elvis spent time with for no apparent reason other than just either to help me out or whatever.

FRED FREDRICK (Classmate and friend)

Elvis realized Thomas Merton's idea that "The pleasure of a good act is something to be remembered—not in order to feed our complacency, but in order to remind us that virtuous actions are not only possible and valuable, but that they can become easier and more delightful and more fruitful than the acts of vice which oppose and frustrate them." He opted for love and life for most of his existence, even though the shadows—overeating and drug abuse—pursued him. Eventually, the darkness of melancholy and the pull of death tipped the balance for Elvis.

24

BEAUTY

Beauty is eternity gazing at itself in a mirror.
But you are eternity and you are the mirror.
KAHLIL GIBRAN

All the world knows beauty
but if that becomes beautiful
this becomes ugly.

LAO TZU

Beautiful words aren't true.

LAO TZU

What we call beautiful or ugly depends on our feelings. Nothing is necessarily beautiful or ugly until feelings make it so. But while feelings differ, they all come from our nature, and we all have the same nature. Hence the sage transforms his feelings and returns to his nature and thus becomes one again.

LU HSI-SHENG (Taoist scholar)

The butterfly is a reminder that life,
though ephemeral, is beautiful.

DENG MING-DAO

Elvis was probably the most handsome, perfect, flawless creature that I had ever laid my eyes on.

JUNE JUANICO

You're beautiful just the way you are.

ELVIS PRESLEY (Speaking to June Juanico)

He was the total androgynous beauty. I would practice Elvis in front of a mirror when I was twelve or thirteen years old.

K. D. LANG (Singer/songwriter)

Elvis was truly an Adonis. But he didn't think himself handsome.

JESS STEARN (American writer)

Beauty is often thought of as one's outer appearance, and in that sense Elvis was beautiful. We usually describe men as handsome, not beautiful, but Elvis had an androgynous beauty. Beauty is also one's inner sacredness, and a beautiful soul can cause an ordinary person to appear outwardly beautiful. Elvis had both inner and outer beauty. Like a mirror, Elvis reflects beauty back to us. The key to lasting beauty is its spirituality, as is reinforced by this Celtic expression: "Only in solitude can you discover a sense of your own beauty." Elvis went a step further when he said, "Silence is the resting place of the soul."

25

NATURE
AND WATER

Water is the source of creation,
the ancestor of all living things.
It's the bloodstream of the Earth.
KUAN-TZU

Express yourself completely,
then keep quiet.
Be like the forces of nature:
when it blows, there is only wind;
when it rains, there is only rain;
when the clouds pass, the sun shines through.

LAO TZU

What is firmly established cannot be uprooted;
What is tightly embraced cannot slip away.

LAO TZU

Nothing in the world is weaker than water
but against the hard and the strong
nothing excels it.

LAO TZU

The Supreme good is like water,
which nourishes all things without trying to.
It is content with the low places that people disdain.
Thus it is like the Tao.

LAO TZU

You've got to have rain in order to have a rainbow.

ELVIS PRESLEY

To Sam Phillips [Elvis] represented the *innocence* that has made the country great in combination with the elements of the soil, the sky, the water, even the wind, the quiet nights... lights up the river—that's what they used to call Memphis. That was where it all came together. And Elvis Presley may not have been able to verbalize that—but he damn sure wasn't dumb, and he damn sure was intuitive, and he damn sure had an appreciation for the spirituality of human existence.... That was what he cared about.

PETER GURALNICK, *Last Train to Memphis*

I found Elvis sitting on the balcony staring out at the ocean. He seemed so solemn. I asked him, "Are you okay?" He said, "Oh, yes, Ma'am. I just can't believe what I'm seeing. I've been sitting here for almost an hour.... I can't believe that it's so big.... I'd give anything in the world if I had enough money to bring my mama and daddy down here to see the ocean."

MAE AXTON

Elvis Presley arrived as *El Niño,* an enormous weather-changing pattern in a culture trying to avoid even the first hints of changing weather.... A culture that both resisted the joyous body, and yearned for it at the same time, created an opening ripe for a soul like Elvis to step through. He would act out the wishes of others, show the way, trail-blaze.

CLARISSA PINKOLA ESTÉS

After Elvis would act and sing, he would retreat and meditate. He would ebb and flow like water, like nature. He represented the dark and wet yin, perfect for the dry and parched yang America of the 1950s. However, like water on a mountaintop, he went down, down, down—eventually into the sea. Yet water gives life; we would die without it.

Now, like a redwood, Elvis is planted deeply in the American soil and psyche as well as being firmly rooted in the Tao. He is here to stay. Forever.

26

WORK (BUSINESS)

When you work you are a flute through whose heart
the whispering of the hours turns to music.

KAHLIL GIBRAN

Work without working.
LAO TZU

He works and does not keep,
When the work is done, he does not tarry with it.
He does not desire to show off his importance to others.
LAO TZU

To live is to work.
DENG MING-DAO

Work for what is lasting.
DENG MING-DAO

When I don't do a good job, I know it and I'm blue as Hell.

ELVIS PRESLEY

Taking Care of Business (TCB) in a flash.

(Elvis's motto and logo "TCB,"
which included a lightning bolt)

[Elvis] came up with a "TCB Oath," too. It said, "more self-respect, more respect for fellow man...Respect for all styles and techniques. Body conditioning, mental conditioning, meditation for calming and stilling of mind and body. Sharpen your skills, and increase mental awareness, for all those who might choose a new outlook and personal philosophy."

LAMAR FIKE

[In 1970, Elvis] played six shows in three days at the Houston Astrodome for $1 million....A total of 208,000 people saw the six shows.

MARTY LACKER

Elvis loved to work hard. He often strove for perfection. He said, "I choose all my own songs…I've gone through more than 100 numbers to get just one that I thought was right." His performances seemed effortless, but behind the natural flow were hours and hours of rehearsals.

Elvis was consumed as part of "the McDonaldization of society." In the 1960s he was efficiently managed as good, clean, and predictable. Elvis projected an all-American image, particularly during his Hollywood years. In that period of making twenty-five films, Elvis was controlled, packaged—and the focus was on quantity, not quality, with "the illusion of intimacy."

Ideally, in a Taoist sense, work is like play, the work of a child. Since Elvis was childlike, his work often was creative play—especially in the early years of his success. After his divorce, in 1973, money became a motivating factor. With his greedy, con-artist, pseudo-colonel manager taking up to 50 percent of Elvis's earnings and gambling away millions, Elvis turned into a workaholic. Besides the drain on his income, Elvis was spending more and more money on his increasing addiction to drugs. In the final five years the childlike joy of work had left him.

27

TRANSCENDENCE
AND
TRANSFORMATION

People who cultivate the Tao are concerned with nothing
except transcending [the] boundaries of life and death.
CH'ENG CHU (Taoist scholar)

To understand yet not understand
is transcendence.

LAO TZU

Those who follow Tao seek to change with it...and
do not hesitate to act in unorthodox ways.

DENG MING-DAO

When the faculties are empty, the heart is full of light.
Being full of light it becomes an influence by which others
are secretly transformed.

CHUANG TZU

Truly, the greatest gift you have to give is that of your own
self-transformation.

LAO TZU

Elvis's life was the truest of American success stories: One day he was a virtual failure, driving a truck for $1.65 an hour and the next day he was on his way to leading a revolution in music and in culture.

DAVID HALBERSTAM (Historian and author of *The Fifties*)

A big part of the problem was that people had put him in a place he couldn't live up to. They just didn't understand that he wasn't a god, he was a man. He carried a very heavy burden—he didn't belong to me, he belonged to the world.

PRISCILLA PRESLEY

Elvis, like America, started out loving, but later turned on himself.

BONO (Lead singer of the band U2)

It was strange that he should have died in the the same month as his mother—and only two days beyond the date on which she died. It was almost as if she had reached out and pulled him through.

LINDA THOMPSON

Transcendence is a step, not a place to get stuck. It can lead to aloofness, inflation, and isolation. Transformation—the next and most important step—results from a union of opposites and leads to something new—it is real and creative change.

Before Elvis recorded "How Great Thou Art," in May of 1966, he said to Larry Geller:

> Millions of people around the world are going to hear this album. It's going to touch people in ways we can't imagine. And I know this album is ordained by God Himself. This is God's message, and I'm His channel. Only I can't be a channel if my ego is there. I have to empty myself so that the channel is totally pure and the message is heard loud and clear. Let's sit down, close our eyes, and meditate. I'm not going to move out of this chair until I'm guided by that still, small voice within.

Larry Geller reports that after they meditated for over half an hour, Elvis said softly, "So be it. I'm ready."

Recording "How Great Thou Art" was a transcendent experience for Elvis. When ten years later he learned that listening to it had saved a woman, named Darlene, from suicide, Elvis was deeply moved. "God works in mysterious ways, that's for sure. If that happened to Darlene, what about others? I mean, a person's life was saved! That's a fulfillment that transcends everything!"

Providing spiritual affirmation of what Elvis thought and felt, the Talmud posits that in the eyes of God, "Whoever saves one life saves the world."

28

SUCCESS
AND FAILURE

You don't have to live in the mountains and forests
or cut yourself off from human affairs to enter the Way.
Success and fame, wealth and honor are all
encouragements to practice.
LIU SHIH-LI (Taoist sage)

When you are deeply into the Way, your virtue is deep;
and when your virtue is deep, then success and honor are
eventually achieved. This is called mysterious virtue. It is
deep, far-reaching, and opposite of ordinary people.

LAO TZU

He does not rejoice in success
Or lament in failure.

CHUANG TZU

Let those who succeed be one with success
let those who fail be one with failure
be one with success
for the Way succeeds too
be one with failure
for the Way fails too.

LAO TZU

The vanity of success invites its own failure.

LAO TZU

Elvis would be nothing, totally unknown, and go into a city and perform, and he would become an instant star before he even left town. It was unreal.

BUDDY KILLEN (Music publisher of "Heartbreak Hotel," Elvis's first million-seller)

It was not only Elvis's deep, exotic voice, bodily gyrations, and musical talent that were responsible for his success. It was also his sense of mission, his rebelliousness, his sexuality, his marginality, his intense struggles with autonomy and dependency.

BRUCE HELLER and ALAN ELMS (Professors of psychology)

Elvis got assassinated in all the fame.

(From Louie Ludwig's The Gospel of Elvis)

Elvis dug his own grave.

BILLY SMITH (Elvis's closest cousin)

Summarizing Elvis's rise and fall, Bruce Heller and Alan Elms wrote, "Rising from rural poverty and obscurity to enormous professional success, Elvis captured the American imagination. Yet in spite of his abilities, his opportunities, and his accomplishments, Elvis never fully realized his creative potential. He was lonely and unhappy most of his life, he failed to establish genuine long-term reciprocal relationships..., and he died at age forty-two from a combination of sustained physical self-neglect and multiple drug abuse."

Elvis ensured that he was both a success and a failure; in a Taoist sense they are the same.

After Lao Tzu stated that "success is as dangerous as failure," he continued:

> What does it mean that success is as dangerous as failure?
> Whether you go up the ladder or down it, your position is shaky.
> When you stand with your two feet on the ground, you will always keep your balance.

The Elvis mirror reflects our own struggle. America is a successful nation, with great prosperity, but we have poverty and hunger, and we are failing with regard to stability of the family, violence, obesity, and other ills from poor diets and sedentary living, as well as drug abuse and addiction.

29

HOME (GRACELAND)

And though of magnificence and splendor, your house
shall not hold your secret nor shelter your longing.
For that which is boundless in you abides in the mansion
of the sky, whose door is the morning mist, and whose
windows are the songs and the silences of night.
KAHLIL GIBRAN

The Tao protects the home.
RICHARD WILHELM
(Chinese scholar
who translated
the *Tao Te Ching*)

Tao is the homeland.
LAO TZU

Houses full of treasure
can never be safe.
LAO TZU

Retreating to hide in secrecy
is eternal calm.
TUNG-PIN LÜ

I only really feel at home in Memphis, at my own "Graceland" mansion. I'll never leave.

ELVIS PRESLEY

My mama was so beautiful and when I'm home back at Graceland, I can feel her presence. I know she's there. I can feel it.

ELVIS PRESLEY

I had never before seen the inside of any house, even in the movies, that was as beautiful and luxurious as Graceland Mansion.

REX MANSFIELD (Army buddy)

It turned out that visiting a dead person's house, no matter who the person was, is an intimate experience. After all, Elvis didn't die in the 1800s. He died in 1977.

MARY PIPHER (Bestselling American author)

Graceland was more than a house; to Elvis it represented "the residence of the heart.... To me my home is all wound up with the acts of kindness and gentleness that my mother and my grandmother and my daddy lovingly provided.... All of this love still remains within its walls. It's an enduring way of life for me."

Graceland is a powerful name and symbol, and Elvis's home is a symbolically integrated *temenos,* or sacred place. Graceland, Elvis's mansion on earth, is like the great mansion in the sky, Heaven. Elvis had always maintained that when he died, he'd be going home. So, in a real way, Paul Simon's song about going to Graceland is like the line of the poet Shinsho: "No matter what road I'm traveling, I'm going home."

Graceland is the site of a yearly candlelight vigil celebrating the anniversary of Elvis's death, on August 16. This spiritual ritual involves entering the gate, walking up the drive to the mansion, and passing in front of Elvis's grave in the Meditation Garden.

30

KING

The king is but a man, as I am;
the violet smells to him as it does to me.
SHAKESPEARE

Use the Tao to help your king.
LAO TZU

The Tao is great
The king is also great.
LAO TZU

Kings would fall if they were always high and noble
thus the noble is based on the humble
the high is founded on the low
thus do kings refer to themselves
as orphaned widowed and destitute
but this is the basis of humility.

LAO TZU

When you realize where you come from,
you naturally become tolerant,
disinterested, amused,
kindhearted as a grandmother,
dignified as a king.
Immersed in the wonder of the Tao,
you can deal with whatever life brings you,
and when death comes,
you are ready.

LAO TZU

I'm not the King... I'm just a singer.

ELVIS PRESLEY

[Elvis] knew exactly who he was. He was the King.

LAMAR FIKE

When the King died holding a book about the shroud of Turin, the entire world has joined in the task of his resurrection.

LOUIE LUDWIG

He was, and remains, the King.

BRUCE HELLER and ALAN ELMS

If you were to ask nearly any American, "Who is the king?" they would respond, "Elvis."

Elvis was trapped by his image, as expressed by Chuang Tzu:

> I looked into your eyes.
> I saw you were hemmed in
> By contradictions.
> You are scared to death,
> You have got lost, and are trying
> To find your way back
> To your own true self.

Regardless, Elvis clearly felt a link to the divine.

31

PAIN AND SUFFERING

And you would watch with serenity
through the winters of your grief. Much of your pain
is self-chosen. It is the bitter potion by which the physician
within you heals your sick self. Therefore trust the physician,
and drink his remedy in silence and tranquillity.

KAHLIL GIBRAN

We ache, because that is human.
To learn from it, that is wisdom.

DENG MING-DAO

One of the hardest things to accept is that disaster has
nothing to do with you.... Misfortunes happen, and we
should face them and act without fear or panic.

DENG MING-DAO

If he gives himself over to extravagance, he will have to
suffer the consequences, with accompanying regret.

I CHING

Clouds and thunder:
The image of difficulty.
Thus the superior man
Brings order out of confusion.

I CHING

The fans, the fans—they don't know my pain.

ELVIS PRESLEY

When you chronicle the demise of Elvis Presley, you have to realize that the tilt started when Gladys died. That was the most devastating thing that ever happened to him. He would never be the same.

LAMAR FIKE

He'd go to great lengths to get pills....This time he dug a hole in his foot...the size of a quarter,...[a] gaping, oozing, bloody, pus hole. I said, "God Almighty, Elvis, what have you done?" And he said, "Bet I get some good stuff now."

MARTY LACKER (With Elvis in a doctor's waiting room)

Those last five years...he was just a tormented person....He didn't know how to stop the drugs. And he didn't want to.

LAMAR FIKE

Late in his life Elvis isolated himself, was very melancholic, and was increasingly in deep pain and suffering. He longed for the abyss—to be unconscious, out of it, and wasted—to escape the suffering. He felt immense agony and grief over the losses of Jesse Garon, his mother, and Priscilla. Elvis's divorce from Priscilla was the most horrific, during and after which he intensified his drug abuse, becoming an addict. It's ironic that after President Richard Nixon made Elvis an honorary federal agent for the Bureau of Narcotics and Dangerous Drugs in 1970, he became what he was supposed to fight. In June of 1976, Elton John had attended one of Elvis's last concerts and later said, "He already seemed like a corpse."

32

HARMONY
AND BALANCE

Perfect harmony is whatever is natural.
LIN HSI-YI (Taoist scholar)

The Tao moves the other way
the Tao works through weakness
the things of this world come from something
something comes from nothing.

LAO TZU

All things have darkness [yin] at their back and strive
towards the light [yang], and the flowing power gives them
harmony.

LAO TZU

Those who cultivate the Way should act with humility and
harmony.... For those who understand that what moves them
is also the source of their life, the pill of immortality is not
somewhere outside.

HUANG YUAN-CHI (Taoist master)

Simply balance the polarities...and...harmony...naturally
arises.

LAO TZU

Gospel music became such a part of my life it was as natural as dancing.

ELVIS PRESLEY

Elvis was harangued by choice; flesh vs. spirit, God vs. rock and roll, mother vs. lover, father vs. Colonel.

BONO

He was a real, complete human being—a combination of good and bad like everyone else.

PRISCILLA PRESLEY

If we make Elvis a saint, we learn nothing from the tragic failures of his life. If we make him an unredeemed sinner, we discount the good of his music, his triumph over abject poverty, his generosity, and his spiritual longings. Balance is the key to appreciating the legacy of Elvis Presley.

RICK STANLEY

When Elvis sang, especially gospel music, he seemed to be in a state of harmony and balance. Late in his life, however, when Elvis was addicted to drugs, he was increasingly in a state of disharmony and imbalance. Little Richard summed up Elvis's plight: "He got what he wanted and lost what he had."

33

PRISONER
AND FREEDOM

The worst imprisonment
is the one we impose on ourselves.
DENG MING-DAO

Care about people's approval
and you will be their prisoner.

LAO TZU

Be content with the moment, and be willing to follow the flow; then there will be no room for grief or joy. In the old days this was called freedom from bondage.

CHUANG TZU

Addiction is most abhorrent to those who follow Tao because it destroys the health of the individual, corrodes the mind, and cuts off freedom.

DENG MING-DAO

He comes very quietly, oppressed in a golden carriage. Humiliation, but the end is reached.

I CHING

What drove us crazy about Elvis wasn't necessarily the sexual freedom his critics claimed he was unleashing, but freedom, period. Freedom to be yourself, to express yourself, to wear what you wanted to wear, to look the way you wanted to look, to have your own style, your own talk.

LARRY GELLER

I know what people think. "Yeah, Elvis is an old recluse like Howard Hughes. He's holed up in his house, he's a prisoner." Bullshit! I love my life. I wouldn't trade my position for anything or anyone. I've earned it. It's what I've always wanted all my life.

ELVIS PRESLEY

The spiritual teachings didn't necessarily change Elvis so much as they gave him a freedom to express his true self. His newfound, or more likely rediscovered, personality was quieter; energetic but not manic; disciplined and more sensitive.

LARRY GELLER

Elvis was like a prisoner. He couldn't get out and do things like other people. Wherever we'd go, people were there; that comes with the territory.

RED WEST (Prior to being fired in 1976, he was a member of Elvis's entourage)

Elvis was an introvert, and all introverts are, in a way, prisoners of themselves. Ironically, he liberated others, though even on stage he could be shy. He broke free and became extraverted through fame and fortune, but then returned to Graceland and his parents. The Army became another kind of prison, as did Hollywood. His marriage was also a trap. Yet the Comeback Special, in 1968, represented a new kind of release because Elvis did it despite the Colonel's opposition. Again, however, he opened doors for others, but shut himself in. The final blow was his drug addiction: He was essentially in solitary confinement after that. Nevertheless, by dying, he freed himself eternally.

34

DESTINY

In a real sense all life is interrelated.
All [people] are caught in an inescapable network
of mutuality, tied in a single garment of destiny.
Dr. Martin Luther King Jr.

Nothing is better than to fulfill your destiny,
but that's the hardest of all.

CHUANG TZU

Find out destiny, govern mental functions,
make preferences orderly and suit real nature.

LAO TZU

Their lives appear miraculous, but all they do is take
advantage of natural events. Timing is everything in Tao.
To act in a way that is harmonious to circumstances and in
accord with one's own heart is rare but precious. Force
doesn't matter. Weight doesn't matter. Even being morally
right doesn't matter. All that matters is timing.... What matters
is the right action at the right time.

DENG MING-DAO

The Master does his job
and then stops.
He understands that the universe
is forever out of control,
and that trying to dominate events
goes against the current of the Tao.

LAO TZU

I always felt that some day, somehow, something would happen to change everything for me.

ELVIS PRESLEY

Elvis saw Jesse's death as an act of God, or destiny. It logically followed that Elvis's living wasn't an accident of fate, either.

LARRY GELLER

I think Elvis often thought he was a prophet. He was very religious....Everything in his life was connected to spirituality....As Elvis got older, he was seeking and searching, and, therefore, in a strange way he became more religious as time went on.

BILL BROWDER

He was destiny's child, but he was never prepared to be what he was.

LAMAR FIKE

Elvis adhered to Lao Tzu's wise words: "The Way is to straighten oneself and await the direction of destiny." In Memphis Elvis recorded two songs for his mother, then waited, seeming to intuitively know that, as Deng Ming-Dao explained: "No one can set out to be a hero. No one can fake being a hero. Being a hero is a matter of being prepared for a gift in time. Time will give you the opening. It is how you then respond that will decide whether you have taken advantage of your opportunity."

35

MEDITATION AND HEALTH

How can I get to know myself?...by meditating.
BEDE GRIFFITHS

When your mind is detached, simple, quiet, then all things can exist in harmony, and you can begin to perceive the subtle truth.

LAO TZU

If you want to see the gods,
just sit down and close your eyes.
DENG MING-DAO

To know peace means to be eternal.
LAO TZU

Those of us who aspire to meditation need only become like a rock. A rock is stable. It knows how to meditate.
DENG MING-DAO

Elvis really took to meditation, and he practiced it daily. In 1964, he decided to create [the] Meditation Garden at Graceland where he, or anyone, could go to be alone, to meditate or to converse in private.

LARRY GELLER

Meditation is better than any drug I know. I can relax, I can breathe deeper, I'm calmer.

ELVIS PRESLEY

Many of his books (including the Bible) said, in so many words, that the body is a temple, to be nourished and cared for, but Elvis overlooked those parts. Intellectually, he knew it was correct, but he figured, what the hell. Anything concerning health invariably fell into one of Elvis's blind spots.

LARRY GELLER

I asked him one time, "Elvis, if you were ever to have anything done in your honor or your memory, what would you like?" He said, "I would like a chapel so my fans would have a place to meditate."

JANELLE MCCOMB (Lifelong friend of Elvis)

Elvis had long-standing practices, such as meditation and reading religious books like *The Prophet,* that helped him detach, relax, and attain a peaceful state of mind. Spiritual music was something else that helped him feel at peace. He once said, "Gospel singing more or less puts your mind to rest. At least it does mine, since I was two."

From the time he was a boy, he was mesmerized by the moon. Lying on a blanket in the middle of the yard, gazing at the full moon and stars, Elvis said to his girlfriend, June Juanico, in 1956, "Keep your eyes on the moon, and you'll see a glowing blue ring appear. [Then], let yourself totally relax, and just focus on the space between the moon and the stars. Don't think about anything! Just let yourself float. If you can relax enough, you can go right up there with them....It takes a little practice, but you can do it if you really want to."

36

MADNESS AND ILLNESS

Which is worse, the madness of following Tao
or the madness of an existence without awareness?
DENG MING-DAO

Only I am so reluctant, I have not yet been given a sign:
like an infant, yet unable to laugh;
unquiet, roving as if I had no home.
All men have abundance, only I am as if forgotten.
I have the heart of a fool: so confused, so dark.
Men of the world are shining, alas, so shining—bright;
only I am as if locked into myself,
unquiet, alas, like the sea,
turbulent, alas, unceasingly.

LAO TZU

The brighter it burns, the quicker it burns out.
YEN TSUN (Taoist sage)

Without controlling how we eat,
we cannot control our existence.
DENG MING-DAO

When illness is overcome, recovery is complete.
DENG MING-DAO

People will come from miles around to see a freak.

ELVIS PRESLEY

Elvis was never the same after his mother died....After the Army...he started taking all this medicine—the pills, the tranquilizers, and sleeping medication like the doctor had him on and prescribed to him immediately following Gladys's death.

ANITA WOOD (One of Elvis's early loves)

On October 9, 1973 [Elvis and Priscilla divorced]. Six days later he was admitted to Baptist Memorial Hospital in Memphis in a semi-comatose condition. He had started having trouble breathing in California and chartered a plane to fly home.... [Eventually Dr. Nichopoulous—better known as Dr. Nick—discovered that] Elvis was getting almost daily injections of Demerol [from a] doctor in California.

PETER GURALNICK (Author of Careless Love)

[After five years of being in "perfect shape" in late] 1975 Elvis starts [to] gain weight and he don't want to show me he is out of shape. I think he shamed himself. The end of 1975 he goes to the hospital, and I lose contact after...His health is going down the hill....He was out of the control....He is locked in his room and he never comes out.

KANG RHEE (Elvis's Memphis karate instructor)

Blessed are the goofballs, the crazies, for they refuse to take things seriously." Rick Stanley said this about Elvis's spontaneous singing of "That's All Right [Mama]" at a break because the song Sam Phillips had asked him to sing, "I Love You Because," wasn't working. Elvis often liked to act silly and crazy. As Larry Geller reported, "He could be wild. His nickname for himself, which he later had inscribed on a bracelet, was Crazy."

Although Elvis's use of sedatives and uppers worsened during the 1960s, it was 1972–74 when his drug use intensified. Larry Geller documented this change, writing, "In addition to his health problems—hypertension, high blood sugar, glaucoma, and a twisted colon that caused him to retain pounds and water weight—[Colonel] Parker's problems [huge debts from compulsive gambling] created stresses for Elvis, adding yet another good 'reason' for him to up his dosages of sedatives, hypnotics, and uppers."

Larry Geller wrote that Elvis once asked him, "Do you think there's a tie-in between medication and meditation?" Elvis grinned, obviously amused by his observation. "It must mean something. It's too similar." Geller admitted, "Sad to say, without medication Elvis wasn't as good, onstage or off, as he was when he had it. There were times when he was more lucid with the drugs than without them. He was an addict."

On January 8, 1975, Elvis spent his fortieth birthday in self-imposed seclusion. Linda Thompson, his girlfriend at the time, characterized Elvis then as "a man suffering from severe depression, someone who...seemed a willing partner in his self-immolation." Sadly, when asked what he thought his

biggest character flaw was, Elvis said, "I'm self-destructive...
but there's not a lot I can do about it."

By his own admission, Elvis felt there was little he could do
to change. Of course, he could have done something, if he'd
only been willing. He could have channeled his rage into
killing his false self, then undergone a symbolic death of his
self-destructive self and rebirth of his creative true self, like the
transformation illustrated in "The King and the Corpse," a
fairy tale from India about the king:

> A decisive triumph on the inner battlefield of the soul
> bestows an essential and thoroughgoing metamor-
> phosis.... The moment [things] change for [the corpse],
> [the king] too is changed. Even the darkness around
> him is transformed into a dawn, glowing with light
> from the Light of the World.

So, what is the meaning of Elvis's kingly struggle?
"Change yourself...and you inherit a renovated world."

Although Elvis did, in part, suffer from madness and illness, diagnosing him with a mental illness would be, in the
words of Lao Tzu, "like pinning a butterfly. The husk is captured, but the flying is lost."

37

COMPASSION AND FORGIVENESS

If you have a heart, you have compassion.
DENG MING-DAO

All people love a compassionate person
as they do their own parents.

WU CH'ENG

I treasure and uphold [compassion]...
because I am compassionate
I can be valiant...
compassion wins every battle
and outlasts every attack
what Heaven creates
let compassion protect.

LAO TZU

Those who are truly [compassionate] are so not because of
theory or ethics, but because they feel the suffering of others
as directly as they would their own.

DENG MING-DAO

Through compassion—that is, identifying with others and
finding the possibilities of their weaknesses within yourself—
you move them to loyalty and gain their obedience.

I CHING

Elvis really always found a way to forgive.

LARRY GELLER

In Monroe, Louisiana, Elvis visited a little girl who was terminally ill. She had written him a letter. Before he went to see her, he got a garnet cross from me which he took out there to the Crippled Children's Hospital and gave to her. He did a lot of neat things like that. Most of the time, no one ever knew.

LOWELL HAYS (Elvis's Memphis jeweler)

Elvis assumed the mantle of family leadership, a role burdened by poverty, lack of social status, his mother's [and father's] alcoholism, his father's prison record [eight months of a three-year sentence for check forgery in Parchman, the Mississippi State penitentiary], and the simple fact that he was a child. If any of his critics need a lesson in compassion, they don't need to look any further than Elvis's childhood to gain respect for what he accomplished.

RICK STANLEY

God, forgive me for my sins. Let... people...have compassion and understanding of the things I have done. Amen.

ELVIS PRESLEY

Compassion means to suffer with the sufferer—Elvis clearly had compassion—and forgiveness is a gift to oneself. However, Elvis may not have fully experienced either until the day before he died. For as Thomas Merton said, "We cannot have true compassion [for] others until we are willing to accept pity and receive forgiveness for our own sins."

38

MIRROR

Elvis presents America
with a face so closely resembling its own
that much of the country can hardly bear
to look in the mirror.
RICK STANLEY

The heart of a wise man is tranquil.
It is the mirror of heaven and earth.

CHUANG TZU

He forgets himself in others,
others forget themselves in him.

TE-CH'ING

Can you wipe your Dark Mirror free of dust?

LAO TZU

Our spirit dwells in our eyes. When the eyes see something
[in the mirror], the spirit chases it. When we close our eyes
and look within, everything is dark. But within the dark, we
still see something. There is still dust. Only by putting an end
to delusions can we get rid of the dust.

WU CH'ENG

They *had* to watch me.

ELVIS PRESLEY

A deeper truth was revealed: "He was like a mirror."

SAM PHILLIPS

We looked at each other move and saw virtual mirror images.

ANN-MARGRET

He was like a wild stallion, just snorting and stomping. And the whole time he was walking on [his] bed he was looking in the mirror...all of a sudden he stopped and said..."I'm a handsome son of a bitch!" And then he died laughing.

JO SMITH (Wife of Elvis's cousin Billy,
recalling Elvis's reaction to being called "fat"
by a rude woman at a theater in 1975)

A favorite Bible verse of Elvis's was 1 Corinthians 13:12, which contains:

> For now we see in a mirror, darkly; but then face to face; now I know in part; but then shall I know even as also I have been known.

Elvis sensed that his image could mirror the Tao or the *imago Dei* (image of God). It is as if Don Miguel Ruiz were writing about Elvis, when he wrote this passage:

> He has discovered that he was a mirror for the use of the people, a mirror in which he could see himself. "Everyone is a mirror," he said. He saw himself in everyone, but nobody saw him as themselves. And he realized that everyone was dreaming, but without awareness, without knowing who they really were. They couldn't see him as themselves because there was a fog or smoke between the mirror.

By viewing Elvis as a mirror, we can develop the "capacity for reflection" about which author Robert Bosnak writes in connection with animated feelings from the magic of earliest childhood. So we, too, can achieve the goal of Taoism: becoming like children again—reborn as our true selves.

Of course, some people see but don't see themselves in the mirror. Elvis saw himself only at the last minute. Sometimes seeing kills you. Regardless, self-forgiveness and forgiveness by a Higher Power is the Way.

39

PURPOSE
AND MEANING

Tao is everything.... A person is part of Tao.
And a person is completely made up of Tao.
DENG MING-DAO

It's important for us to have goals and to strive toward them with the valor and the determination of the carp. Those of us who have goals have meaning and direction in our lives.... Just as the carp will swim against the current to reach its goal, so too must we know when we must stand up to fate in order to be successful.

DENG MING-DAO

When you do something, don't hold back. Shoot it all, go for it all.... To be with Tao is to live a creative life. To live a creative life always means that you express who you are.

DENG MING-DAO

Other people are bright;
I alone am dark.
Other people have a purpose;
I alone don't know.

LAO TZU

Because he has no goal in mind,
everything he does succeeds.

LAO TZU

I've always known that there had to be a purpose for my life. I've always felt an unseen hand behind me, guiding my life.

ELVIS PRESLEY

There's a meaning for everything....I always knew there was a *real* spiritual life.

ELVIS PRESLEY

All I knew was, the only way to do it, the only way to make it, what got me to this point, was to just be natural and let it happen. And don't stop. The minute I started thinking, it would turn off. So, you don't think. Just do. Just be.

ELVIS PRESLEY

For someone like Elvis, who had wondered where he fit into the scheme of things, what his purpose might be, what meaning lay behind the improbable and extraordinary events in his life, a passage such as this [from *The Impersonal Life*] spoke [to him] very clearly: "When you have found The Kingdom, you will likewise find your place in It, realizing...that your work was all laid out for you from the beginning, and that all that has gone before has been but a preparation and a fitting of your human personality for that work."

In the years to come, Elvis always kept a copy of *The Impersonal Life* with him wherever he went and gave away hundreds of copies to others.

LARRY GELLER

Elvis felt he was born for a purpose that was amplified twofold because of his twin's death.

Larry Geller noted that "the culmination of his readings and his involvement with the Self-Realization [Fellowship] made [Elvis] feel quite strongly that he was chosen to help humanity, to carry a message."

In the margins of one of Elvis's favorite books, *Letters of Helena Roerich,* he wrote, "Self-purification will clear our path and make [the] understanding better [of] our purpose."

40

PRAYER AND SACRIFICE

Each one prays to God according to his own light
[and] the world is touched by sacrifice.
MAHATMA GANDHI

Prayer is a form of meditation. It is an act of reflection.

DENG MING-DAO

We are moved to pray, not because we want something, but because we are moved to devotion over the presence of Tao.

DENG MING-DAO

The gods... will test our willingness to sacrifice and reach the other side of enlightenment instead of succumbing to greed and our own degradation.

KWAN SAIHUNG

Heaven and Earth are not benevolent. To them men are like straw dogs destined for sacrifice.

LAO TZU

I cried out to God, "If that's really me, Lord, I want to die. All I truly want is you. Please, God, fill me with yourself. Destroy me, if that's what it takes."

ELVIS PRESLEY

I took both his hands in mine and said, "Elvis, right now I want to pray for you." He said, "Please do," and started weeping.

REX HUMBARD (Televangelist, with Elvis after his last performance in Las Vegas, December 12, 1976)

He felt like Jesus betrayed by his disciples.

PETER GURALNICK, *Careless Love* (Commenting on Elvis's reaction to the book *Elvis: What Happened?*, published the year he died, by Red and Sonny West and Dave Hebler as told to Steve Dunleavy)

Dear Lord, please show me a way. I'm tired and confused, and I need your help.

ELVIS PRESLEY (One of his prayers the night he died, recorded by Rick Stanley)

A devotedly spiritual person, Elvis prayed and in a real way sacrificed himself so he could join his mother in Heaven. The archetypal Elvis remains a kingly hero. As Zimmer said, "The king's way leads from earthly pomp, through realms of death, to the summit of glory. The empty attitude of kingly splendor—brittle and doomed—contained within itself the seed of death; but the way of death is itself the way of initiation. The fiends of the grave reach out with a ghostly grip at the throat, and the life forfeited to death is broken on the rack; nevertheless, the end is life reborn, with exemption from death forever, self-entirety and consecration."

41

DEATH
AND REBIRTH

Estranged and re-united the new Being.
PAUL TILLICH (Existentialist philosopher)

Daring to act means death.
                    LAO TZU

The strong do not die a natural death.
                    LAO TZU

Going out is life, going in is death.
                    LAO TZU

Who uses his light
who trusts his vision
lives beyond death
this is the Hidden Immortal.
                    LAO TZU

Don't forget, angels fly because they take themselves so lightly.

ELVIS PRESLEY (His last words to Larry
Geller, before he died)

I'm not afraid of death. Only the ignorant, the unenlightened person is afraid of death.

ELVIS PRESLEY

The soul's free. The soul is going back to God, going home again.

ELVIS PRESLEY

I'm not surprised that people want him alive, but Elvis Presley was laid to rest on August 18, 1977. He will live forever.

LARRY GELLER

Twelve days before Elvis died, he telephoned Larry Geller at his home in California and said, "If you didn't help me on the spiritual path, I would've been dead years ago. You know, we have to leave on the sixteenth and I really need you here."

Larry responded, "Don't worry, Elvis, I'll be there."

Elvis then said, "Look, Larry, I'm on fire, man. Why me, Lord, why me?" He then reminded Larry, "Don't forget to get me the best book on the Holy Shroud of Jesus. I really need to look into it. It seems that it's definite proof that Jesus…did walk the earth and for some reason left behind His own cloth that they wrapped His body in that made His imprint. His spirit. The Christ is eternal and now we have physical proof."

Elvis felt that there was a relationship between himself and Christ. Nearly ten years after Elvis's religious experience in the desert, he shared a secret with Larry Geller: "I, ah, ah…I wanna tell you something. Cause, ah, you're the only person who could possibly understand…when I had that experience in the desert. I didn't only see Jesus' picture in the clouds—Jesus Christ literally exploded in me. Larry, it *was* me! I *was* Christ…I swear to God, Larry, I thought I might be him…Elvis Christ, Jesus Christ…I stood alone, Larry. I had a secret.…All I had were my prayers. I said many times, 'Lord, if you want me, if I'm the one, You gotta show me. Cause by myself, I'm lost. And if I'm wrong, if I'm not what I suspect, then show me, give me strength.'"

Many criticize Elvis for his grandiose and strange ideas—for example, claiming that he was a Christ-like figure. Regardless, it's important (if not vital) for us to have compassion for the human Elvis and adhere to the words of C. W. Bradley, who gave a beautiful and honest eulogy at Elvis's funeral:

"Elvis was a frail human being. And he would be the first to admit his weaknesses. Elvis would not want anyone to think that he had no fears or faults. But now that he's gone, I find it more helpful to remember his good qualities, and I hope you do, too."

The archetypal Elvis leaves a powerful imprint of his own spirit and soul, as well as the Tao that operates through him. Larry Geller's observation rings true: "It is as if Elvis never really left us, and in a sense that is true, for his image, his music, and the force of his personality remain. Through his greatness, his fans' love and a once-in-a-lifetime confluence of circumstances, he evolved into a reflection not only of our hopes and dreams, but of our struggles and weaknesses."

The death and rebirth motif, associated with Elvis, continues to evolve—this is the mysterious Tao of Elvis.

42

SPIRITUAL WHOLENESS

Pray to roundness; Wholeness. The cycle of the moon,
the seasons. We thank the Great Creator for the new life
and for the life it sprang from. The past and future,
cinched together. The roundness of things.

WALLY LAMB

One is the beginning and end of things. All things become complete when they become one.

WANG PI (Taoist scholar)

Tao is creation's sanctuary.
LAO TZU

The kingly man's glory is in knowing
That all things come together in One
And that life and death are equal.
CHUANG TZU

The universe is a harmonious Oneness.
LAO TZU

God has a reason for everything. We just have to fit the pieces together.

ELVIS PRESLEY

Our soul, our life force, goes on when the body dies. We have nothing to fear; God will take the last journey with us.

ELVIS PRESLEY

Once I go, the world is going to really start changing. That's when it will all start.

ELVIS PRESLEY

As Jennifer was dying, she seemed to light up. The light looked as though it were coming from within her. She smiled a big smile. She was looking upwards and holding her arms out like she was trying to reach toward and hug someone. She said it twice, "Here comes Elvis." Then she collapsed and died.

SHERRY REED (Interviewed by Dr. Raymond Moody
for Elvis After Life. This is what she said upon
the death of her eleven-year-old daughter)

Spiritual Wholeness, the Tao, and Oneness all represent the totality of the psyche and cosmos. A person who wishes "to cultivate Tao [the Oneness], must first know Tao [the Oneness]."

In Taoism, death and birth are equal. As Lao Tzu said, "The Way gave birth to Unity," and in death, one returns to Unity and the Way, or Tao. Rousselle echoes this sentiment: "Our true essential nature is the 'primal spirit' in which nature and life are one, it is the great divine Tao...the great One." Remember what Lao Tzu said about the Tao: "It turns in a circle and does not endanger itself."

The Tao of Elvis is the essence of Elvis.
"[He] who dies but doesn't perish lives on."
ELVIS LIVES!

NOTES

PREFACE

ix   *"Elvis Presley is the greatest"*   Higgins, p. 66.

ix   *"I love Elvis and hope"*   http://www.elvis-presley.com/HTML/elviso_q_about.html.

x   *The Tao, a mysterious force*   Rosen (1997), p. 23.

x   *evolution of the psyche*   book by Rosen and Luebbert.

x   *"archetypes and the collective unconscious"*   Jung (1968), pp. 42–43.

xi   *"This is the profound, simple truth"*   Lao Tzu (1992a), p. 48.

xi   *"the force of God"*   Geller, p. 66.

xi   *"Free from care"*   Chuang Tzu (1992), p. 196.

xii   *"But he had insight"*   Ming-Dao (1993), p. 474.

xii   *prefigured the civil rights movement*   Early, G. This view is shared by Calvin Newborn, an African-American blues guitarist in Memphis, who knew Elvis as a teenager when he used to visit clubs on Beale Street. See *Why Elvis?*, a documentary by David Leonard, 1994, Kulter.

xii   *"In Elvis white Americans"*   Walker, pp. 187–188.

xii   *When Elvis's Scotch-Irish and Jewish . . .* see Dundy.

xii   *central to his spiritual life*   Read by Elvis at home and on tour: *The Prophet,* by Kahlil Gibran; *The Impersonal Life,* by Joseph Benner; *Autobiography of a Yogi,* by Paramahansa Yogananda; and the *Holy Bible,* especially the Old Testament, or Torah. For a complete listing of Elvis's spiritual books, see the appendix in *If I Can Dream,* by Geller, pp. 325–328.

xii   *Self-Realization Fellowship*   In Guralnick (1999), there are eight references to the Self-Realization Fellowship, which was founded by Yogananda and after his death, in 1952, run by his disciple Faye Wright (Sri Daya Mata), who was an important figure to Elvis. Guralnick (1999) makes eleven references to Faye Wright.

xiii *Elvis is everywhere* book by Scherman. Also Mojo Nixon and Skid Roper's song by the same name is a humorous but serious mythic hymn, "Elvis is Everywhere," Bo-Day-Shus album, Enigma Records, 1987.

xiii *Muhammad Ali* Miller. It is made clear in this book that Muhammad Ali is a very spiritual person who, like Elvis, has the Tao working through him. It is understandable that when they met, they liked each other, and gave each other gifts.

xiii *"Sightings" are almost* See Eicher.

xiii *In 1998, twenty-one* Pareles, sec. E, p. 5.

xiii *"Before Elvis there was nothing"* Higgins, p. 12.

xiv The Tao of Elvis *is a psychological and philosophical work* Philosophy derives from *philo*, which means friend, and *sophia*, which means wisdom. Sophia is also known as the mother of God, another parallel with the Tao, which is matriarchal.

xv *"When we were kids"* Higgins, p. 48.

xvi *At this meeting I failed* Someday I'll write about this in more detail. Subsequently, I took it again and passed without difficulty.

xvi *I decided to write* This book is about the Elvis mirror and how the Tao of Elvis touches one deeply on a spiritual level, it is not a biography of Elvis Presley. For the best biography see the definitive two volumes by Peter Guralnick.

INTRODUCTION

xvii *"All I ever wanted"* Geller, p. 233.

xvii *"Elvis Presley's death"* http://www.elvis-presley.com/HTML/elviso_q_about.html.

xviii *"a symbol of the country's vitality"* Brown and Broeske, p. 42.

xviii *"Encouraging others"* Lao Tzu (1992a), p. 106.

xviii *"Elvis Presley was more"* Higgins, p. 56.

xviii *"When I first heard"* Higgins, p. 42.

xviii *"egocide and transformation"* Rosen (2002), pp. xxi–xxviii, 61–84.

xviii *the Memphis Mafia* The name of Elvis's entourage, usually twelve male members, made up of friends, companions, and bodyguards.

xix *"A woman ran down"* Sumner in Haining, p. 147.

xix *"Elvis is loved, he is hated"* Higgins, p. 161.

xx *"There ain't nothing"* Farren, p. 89.

xxi *"Don't go crazy"* Lao Tzu (1992a), p. 55.

xxi *Elvis was intensely, even* According to Carl Jung, a man's anima (soul or feminine side) evolves through contact with: (1) *mother*. During boyhood; women are seen as caretakers who love unconditionally; (2) *lover*. During adolescence; women are seen primarily as sexual, an opportunity for physical merging; (3) *equal partner*. In the later years; women are seen as equals, which allows for adult relationships, marriage, and genuine friendship; (4) *spiritual wise old woman*. As men age, women are experienced as mature beings and spiritual companions. Elvis (like our society) was (is) stuck in the first and second levels. Jung (1966a), pp. 188–211.

xxi   *"Sex [is] not the answer"*   Whitmer, p. 419.

xxii   *was he a sacrificial dying god*   Estés, pp. 19–20, 22.

xxii   *a book on the shroud of Jesus*   This book, *The Scientific Search for the Face of Jesus,* by Frank O. Adams, was brought to Elvis by his spiritual adviser, Larry Geller. Geller, p. 303.

xxiii *"Superior people can awaken"*   Lao Tzu (1992a), p. 98.

xxiii *"kept out of heaven"*   Nash, p. 3

1: TAO

1   *"Elvis thought the"*   Larry Geller, interview by author, 1999.

2   *"The Tao does"*   Lao Tzu (1996), p. 74.

2   *"Before Heaven and Earth"*   Lao Tzu (1985), No. 25, p. 37.

2   *"The Master doesn't take"*   Lao Tzu (1988), No. 5.

2   *"It is a movement"*   Ming-Dao (1993), p. 202.

3   *"I'm a soul"*   Guralnick (1999), p. 222.

3   *"You know, one"*   Ibid., p. 205.

3   *"Elvis could be"*   Stanley, pp. 180–181.

3   *"Elvis was both"*   Ibid., pp. 203 and 190.

4   *"Mystery of mysteries"*   Lao Tzu (1990), No. 1, p. 59.

4   *"I know now."*   Geller, p. 114.

4   *"A monk should"*   Heiler in Campbell (1960), p. 195.

4   *"the great Tao"*   Rousselle in Campbell (1960), p. 96.

2: OPPOSITES

5   *"Elvis's music and his personality"*   http://www.elvis-presley.com/ HTML/elviso_q_about.html

6   *"Know the male"*   Lao Tzu (1988), No. 28.

6   *"The Tao doesn't"*   Ibid., No. 5.

6   *"Know the white"*   Ibid., No. 28.

6   *"The bright Way"*   Lao Tzu (1990), No. 41, p. 7.

7   *"You accept the bad"*   Farren, p. 90.

7   *"Elvis would bounce"*   Nash, p. 375.

7   *"It's not black"*   Guralnick (1994), p. 99.

7 "Elvis has a kindred spirit"   Ibid., pp. 134–135.
8 "The bottom line"   Stanley, p. 190.
8 "Contradiction is given"   Buber in Campbell (1960), p. 184.

3: CHILD

9 "The great man"   Lao Tzu (1996), p. 56.
10 "He who is"   Lao Tzu (1988), No. 55.
10 "Can you make"   Lao Tzu (1985), No. 10, p. 30.
10 "My bond with"   Chuang Tzu (1992), p. 172.
10 "Don't lose your"   Lao Tzu (1996), p. 56.
11 "From the time"   Farren, p. 35.
11 "Elvis grew up"   Guralnick (1994), p. 13.
11 "My total image"   Ibid., p. 120.
11 "Elvis was always"   Stanley, p. 171.
12 "Those who possess"   Lao Tzu (1996), p. 61.
12 During the last   Nash, pp. 539, 618–619.

4: MOTHER

13 "People are born"   Lao Tzu (1996), p. 105.
14 "Who knows the"   Ibid., p. 104.
14 "I have the"   Lao Tzu (1985), No. 20, p. 35.
14 "The female is"   Lao Tzu (1996), p. 122.
14 "Children are no"   Ibid., p. 104.
15 "I love you"   Geller, p. 47.
15 "Losing my mother"   Farren, pp. 30–31.
15 "He was a mama's boy"   Guralnick (1994), p. 36.
15 "Elvis was not a 'mama's boy'"   Juanico, p. 162.
16 "He was white as"   Nash, p. 137.
16 "Elvis never really"   Stanley, p. 190.
16 Five months before he died   Geller, pp. 229–230.
16 "Son, our love"   Ibid., p. 230.
16 "I'll never leave"   Ibid.

5: FATHER

17 "And how shall"   Gibran, p. 52.
18 "No one understands"   Lao Tzu (1996), p. 104.
18 "When a hideous"   Chuang Tzu (1992), p. 116.
18 "The wise look"   Ming-Dao (1996), p. 197.

18 *"When people are"*   Lao Tzu (1996), p. 144.

19 *"I made my"*   Farren, p. 17.

19 *"Elvis loved his"*   Clayton, p. 225.

19 *"The Colonel is"*   Farren, p. 80.

19 *"I picked up"*   Ann H. Finch, interview by author, 1996.

20 *"very often produces"*   Jung in Campbell (1954), p. 10.

6: FAMILY AND FRIENDS

21 *"Family and friends"*   Carleton's, p. 62.

22 *"Honor your parents"*   Lao Tzu (1992a), p. 64.

22 *"The first practice"*   Ibid., p. 4.

22 *"We cannot be"*   Ming-Dao (1996), p. 127.

22 *"When you think"*   Ibid., p. 89.

23 *"I was raised"*   Farren, p. 107.

23 *"Elvis treated me better"*   Clayton, p. 124.

23 *"Elvis was an enormously"*   Ibid., p. 278.

23 *"We were all"*   Guralnick (1999), p. 217.

24 *psychologist Erik Erikson*   See Erikson (1982).

24 *"a great capacity for friendship"*   Jung (1968), p. 86.

7: SPIRIT, SOUL, AND RELIGION

25 *"You have walked"*   Gibran, p. 9.

26 *"The world is"*   Lao Tzu (1996), p. 58.

26 *"Can you educate"*   Lao Tzu (1985), No. 10, p. 30.

26 *"To arrive"*   Lao Tzu (1992a), p. 50.

26 *"Everything we do"*   Ming-Dao (1996), p. 15.

27 *"I always knew"*   Geller, p. 51.

27 *"Elvis was pure"*   Clayton, p. 340.

27 *"Elvis is becoming"*   Nash, p. 339.

27 *"The Gospel of Elvis"*   Ludwig, pp. 144–145, 107–108.

28 *"Elvis often spoke"*   Ann H. Finch, interview by author, 1996.

28 *"Often he is endowed"*   Jung (1968), p. 87.

8: LOVE

29 *"Much have we"*   Gibran, p. 9.

30 *"Through love one"*   Lao Tzu (1985), No. 67, p. 58.

30 *"Kindness in giving"*   Lao Tzu (1970), p. 18.

30 *"Love your life"*   Lao Tzu (1992a), p. 106.

30 *"The deeper the"* Lao Tzu (1996), p. 88.

31 *"My moment of"* Geller, p. 233.

31 *"Elvis was sweet"* Clayton, p. 11.

31 *"Elvis had a great"* Ibid., p. 319.

31 *"Everyone knew Elvis"* Stanley, p. 148.

32 *"My love for Lisa"* Geller, p. 297.

32 *"It's like a surge"* Guralnick (1999), p. 315.

32 love's twin, *"strife"* Stevens, p. 12. Stevens linked strife to Freud's thanatos, the power of death, which is contrary to its opposite, eros, the pull of love and life.

32 *"For even as"* Gibran, p. 12.

32 *"All that a man"* Iyer (1992), frontispiece.

9: MUSIC AND SONG

33 *"Music is the"* Edwards, p. 430.

34 *"A good artist"* Lao Tzu (1988), No. 27.

34 *"Hold up the Great"* Lao Tzu (1996), p. 70.

34 *"Performed with the harmony"* Chuang Tzu (1994), pp. 133, 135–136.

34 *"When the center"* Ibid., p. 149.

35 *"My voice is"* Guralnick (1994), p. 331.

35 *"Elvis sang songs"* Ibid., p. 79.

35 *"He was really"* Ibid., p. 151.

35 *"There was a floating"* Ibid., p. 205

36 *"I feel God"* Guralnick (1999), p. 223. Listening to "Amazing Grace," RCA (two compact discs of Elvis's greatest sacred performances of fifty-five gospel songs) is quite convincing.

36 *"I forget myself"* in Yogananda (1998), p. 262.

36 *"How Great Thou Art"* Elvis received two Grammy awards for this hymn. He received a third Grammy for another spiritual song, and a fourth Grammy for his lifetime achievements as a creative artist.

10: GRACE AND GENTLENESS

37 *"Simple grace"* I Ching (1967), pp. 93, 221.

38 *"The man"* Chuang Tzu (1992), p. 137.

38 *"Gentleness"* Lao Tzu (1992a), p. 63.

38 *"With gentleness"* I Ching (1982), p. 14.

38 *"Make your mood"* Lü, p. 31.

39 *"All good flows"* Written, during the last year of Elvis's life, in the

margin of page 265 of one of his favorite books, *Letters of Helena Roerich,* published in 1939 by the Agni Yoga Society (a photocopy of the page was provided by Larry Geller).

39 "Elvis was a"   Guralnick (1994), p. 16.

39 *"His small child's"*   Ibid., p. 22.

39 *"Elvis never had"*   Clayton, p. 121.

40 *"One feels it a grace"*   Heschel, p. 33.

40 *"Possession in great measure"*   I Ching (1967), p. 60.

11: DARKNESS, SORROW, AND SADNESS

41 *"Where there is sorrow"*   Edwards, p. 632.

42 *"The one we call dark"*   Lao Tzu (1996), p. 2.

42 *"The birth of a man"*   Chuang Tzu (1992), p. 147.

42 *"Inside there is"*   Lao Tzu (1996), p. 42.

42 *"The brightest path"*   Ibid., p. 82.

43 *"[Elvis was] a sad"*   Guralnick (1994), p. 26.

43 *"Elvis always seemed"*   Ann H. Finch, interview by author, 1996.

43 *"I've made a"*   Guralnick (1994), pp. 323–324.

43 *"I felt sorry"*   Guralnick (1999), p. 488.

44 *"The Tao, the dark"*   Lao Tzu (1996), p. xi.

44 *"The Tao is dark and"*   Lao Tzu (1988), No. 21.

12: LIGHT, FIRE, AND PASSION

45 *"The passions are"*   Edwards, p. 467.

46 *"In the deep"*   Chuang Tzu (1992), p. 109.

46 *"The light itself"*   Lü, p. 15.

46 *"In passion we"*   Lao Tzu (1996), p. 2.

46 *"Where the fountains"*   Chuang Tzu (1992), p. 89.

47 *"Send me some"*   Geller, p. 211.

47 *"I'm afraid I'll"*   Guralnick (1994), p. 269.

47 *"He's just a"*   Clayton, p. 69.

47 *"Music ignited a"*   Guralnick (1999), p. 149.

48 *"Light does not"*   Lao Tzu (1996), p. 57.

48 *"The face of God"*   Guralnick (1999), p. 628.

13: DREAMS

49 *"Your youth has"*   Gibran, p. 8.

50 *"Life is like"*   Ming-Dao (1996), p. 230.

50 *"Dreams are the"*   Lü, p. 15.

50 *"Once upon a"* Chuang Tzu (1974), p. 48.
50 *"By and by"* Ibid., p. 45.
51 *"My whole life"* Clayton, p. 44. *"I hope I"* Farren, p. 17.
51 *"I was running"* Juanico, pp. 224–225.
51 *"My life's"* Clayton, p. 260.
51 *"It's like Elvis"* Higgins, p. 114.
52 *"Elvis and Lisa Marie"* Geller, pp. 292–293.
52 *"it shows the inner truth"* Jung (1966b), p. 142.

14: GIVING AND GENEROSITY

53 *"See first that"* Gibran, p. 23.
54 *"The more he"* Lao Tzu (1996), p. 162.
54 *"He is humane"* Lao Tzu (1992b), No. 16, p. 23.
54 *"When first one"* Ming-Dao (1996), p. 132.
54 *"He gives his"* Lao Tzu (1996), p. 163.
55 *"I'm so lucky"* Geller, p. 281.
55 *"Elvis was always"* Clayton, p. 214.
55 *"You're giving"* Ibid., p. 214.
55 *"Elvis was the"* Ibid., p. 262.
56 *"Elvis had a special way"* Dr. Lester Hofman, interview by author, 1996.
56 *"I know I drove"* Guralnick (1999), p. 550.

15: ALONE AND LONELINESS

57 *"As soon as"* Merton, p. 113.
58 *"What men hate"* Lao Tzu (1985), No. 42, p. 46.
58 *"All spirituality"* Ming-Dao (1996), p. 200.
58 *"Other people are"* Lao Tzu (1988), No. 20.
58 *"To live the life"* Ming-Dao (1996), p. 234.
59 *"People think I'm"* Geller, p. 13.
59 *"Elvis was a"* Clayton, p. 28.
59 *"I get lonesome"* Farren, p. 10.
59 *"Elvis was an"* Guralnick (1999), p. 560.
60 *"I swear to God"* Geller, p. 34.
60 *"The king is always killed"* Pearlman, p. 142.

16: TWINNING AND PAIRING

61 *"Whether laughing or"* Shimano, p. 98.
62 *"The coexistence of"* Lao Tzu (1996), p. 4.

62 *"So everything we"* Ming-Dao (1996), p. 217.

62 *"The existence of things"* Lao Tzu (1996), p. 4.

62 *"[Tao] causes being"* Chuang Tzu (1992), p. 183.

63 *"They say when"* Geller, p. 37.

63 *"As Elvis's life"* Whitmer, p. 139.

63 *"[At] the funeral"* Clayton, pp. 217–218.

63 *"I dreamed that"* Guralnick (1999), pp. 582–583.

17: MAN OF TAO

65 *"All those who"* Ming-Dao (1996), p. 216.

66 *"The Man of"* Lao Tzu (1985), No. 7, p. 29.

66 *"Thus also...he encompasses"* Ibid., No. 22, p. 36.

66 *"Thus also...he sets"* Ibid., No. 58, p. 53.

66 *"Whoever knows himself"* Ibid., No. 33, p. 41.

67 *"Man, all I"* Geller, p. 23.

67 *"Elvis was just"* Guralnick (1994), pp. 68, 79.

67 *"Elvis came in"* Clayton, p. 45.

67 *"Elvis's love for"* Ibid., p. 128.

68 *"Elvis...was a man...who truly"* Guralnick (1999), pp. 85–86.

68 *"Lao Tzu extols"* Lao Tzu (1996), p. 66.

18: INNOCENCE AND PLAY

69 *"Verily the ocean"* Gibran, p. 48.

70 *"In innocence we"* Lao Tzu (1996), p. 2.

70 *"Innocence is inside"* Ming-Dao (1996), p. 244.

70 *"Innocence does not"* Ibid., p. 31.

70 *"Playing is as"* Ibid., p. 144.

71 *"Elvis looked like"* Juanico, p. 47.

71 *"Elvis was always"* Clayton, p. 11.

71 *"Elvis didn't radiate"* Geller, p. 323.

71 *"It didn't matter"* Clayton, p. 72.

72 *"Innocence and passion"* Lao Tzu (1996), p. 3.

72 *"This [God-given]"* Cammerloher, p. 431.

19: KNOWLEDGE AND WISDOM

73 *"Reading gives God"* Merton, p. 62.

74 *"Mastering books is"* Ming-Dao (1996), p. 38.

74 *"Knowing others is"* Lao Tzu (1988), No. 33.

74 *"For he who"* quoted in Chuang Tzu (1992), p. 177.
74 *"Tao is the"* Ming-Dao (1996), p. 137.
75 *"A long time ago"* Juanico, pp. 250, 314–315.
75 *"Although it hardly"* Geller, p. 49.
75 *"He had incredible"* Guralnick (1999), p. 463.
75 *"I have my"* Ibid., p. 135.
76 *"Knowledge comes with"* Harvey, p. 32.
76 *"He remained a"* Geller, p. 51.
76 *"Wisdom laughs to"* Harvey, p. 208.

20: IMAGE (PERSONA AND SHADOW)

77 *"Your shadow has"* Gibran, p. 9.
78 *"Whoever holds fast"* Lao Tzu (1985), No. 35, p. 42.
78 *"If a man"* Chuang Tzu (1992), p. 94.
78 *"Image refers to"* Lao Tzu (1996), p. 43.
78 *"The Great Image"* Ibid., p. 70.
79 *"The image is"* Higgins, p. 14.
79 *"They know about"* Geller, p. 215.
79 *"No one can"* Ibid., p. 14.
79 *"The interesting thing"* Ibid., p. 32.
80 *"They don't know me"* Whitmer, p. 404.
80 *"Do you realize"* Geller, p. 233.
80 *"He taught me"* Higgins, p. 88.

21: TRUTH AND TRUTH OF CHARACTER

81 *"What is true"* Lao Tzu (1996), p. 162.
82 *"The truest truth"* Lao Tzu (1996), p. 82.
82 *"In public, we"* Ming-Dao (1996), p. 204.
82 *"You have got"* Chuang Tzu (1992), p. 193.
82 *"Those who want"* Lao Tzu (1992a), p. 63.
83 *"I knew in"* Geller, p. 40.
83 *"Son,... always remember"* Clayton, p. 25.
83 *"There is something"* http://www.elvis-presley.com/HTML/
elviso_q_about.html
83 *"Elvis...was [a]"* Clayton, p. 378.
84 *"Insist on yourself"* Kabat-Zinn, p. 210.
84 *"That the truth"* Guralnick (1999), p. 175.

22: HAPPINESS AND JOY

85 *"Your joy is"* Gibran, pp. 32–33

86 *"To increase life"* Lao Tzu (1985), No. 55, p. 52.

86 *"You never find"* Chuang Tzu (1992), p. 149.

86 *"If you practice"* Ibid., p. 150.

86 *"Happiness rests on"* Lao Tzu (1985), No. 58, p. 53.

87 *"Someone to love"* Nash, p. 553.

87 *"Elvis had a"* Clayton, p. 260.

87 *"Elvis was one"* Geller, p. 96.

87 *"It's... important"* Guralnick (1999), p. 136.

88 "A flame to melt" Melville, p. 144.

88 *"From joy I came"* Yogananda, p. 146.

23: VIRTUE

89 *"The reason people"* Lao Tzu (1996), p. 141.

90 *"The Way begets"* Ibid., p. 102.

90 *"Cultivated in the self"* Ibid., p. 108.

90 *"He who contains"* Ibid., p. 110

90 *"The virtue of"* Ibid., p. 136.

91 *"Elvis was good"* Clayton, pp. 23, 383.

91 *"He felt he had"* Guralnick (1994), p. 337.

91 *"Elvis came out"* Higgins, p. 20.

91 *"I admired Elvis"* Clayton, p. 36.

92 *"The pleasure"* Merton, p. 31.

24: BEAUTY

93 *"Beauty is eternity"* Gibran, p. 83

94 *"All the world"* Lao Tzu (1996), p. 4.

94 *"Beautiful words"* Ibid., p. 162.

94 *"What we call"* Ibid., p. 4.

94 *"The butterfly is"* Ming-Dao (1996), p. 229.

95 *"Elvis was probably"* Clayton, p. 69.

95 *"You're beautiful"* Juanico, p. 69.

95 *"He was the total"* http://www.elvis-presley.com/HTML/elviso_q_about.html.

95 *"Elvis was truly"* Stearn, p. 17.

96 *"Only in solitude"* O'Donohue, p. 135.

96 *"Silence is the"* Guralnick (1999), p. 456.

25: NATURE AND WATER

97 *"Water is the source"* Lao Tzu (1996), p. 16.

98 *"Express yourself"* Lao Tzu (1988), No. 23.

98 *"What is firmly"* Lao Tzu (1990), No. 54, p. 23.

98 *"Nothing in the world"* Lao Tzu (1996), p. 86.

98 *"The Supreme good"* Lao Tzu (1988), No. 8.

99 *"You've got to"* Juanico, p. 75.

99 *"To Sam Phillips [Elvis] represented"* Guralnick (1994), p. 121.

99 *"I found Elvis"* Clayton, p. 69; Guralnick (1994), p. 186. Daytona Beach, Florida, 7 May 1955, during Elvis's first trip to Florida. Mae Axton gave Elvis early concert exposure in Florida, co-wrote "Heartbreak Hotel," and saw to it that he brought his folks to Florida to see the ocean. She and Elvis remained friends for the rest of his life.

99 *"Elvis Presley arrived"* Estés, pp. 37, 39.

26: WORK (BUSINESS)

101 *"When you work"* Gibran, p. 27.

102 *"Work without working"* Lao Tzu (1996), p. 126.

102 *"He works and"* Lao Tzu (1985), No. 77, p. 62.

102 *"To live is"* Ming-Dao (1996), p. 110.

102 *"Work for what"* Ibid., p. 113.

103 *"When I don't"* Farren, p. 27.

103 *"Taking Care of"* Brown, p. 353.

103 *"[Elvis] came up"* Nash, pp. 481–482.

103 *"[In 1970, Elvis]"* Ibid., p. 483.

104 *"I choose all"* Guralnick (1999), p. 143.

104 *"the McDonaldization of Society"* Ritzer.

104 *"the illusion of intimacy"* Ibid., pp. 100, 113.

27: TRANSCENDENCE AND TRANSFORMATION

105 *"People who cultivate"* Lao Tzu (1996), p. 100.

106 *"To understand yet"* Ibid., p. 142.

106 *"Those who follow"* Ming-Dao (1996), p. 65.

106 *"When the faculties"* Chuang Tzu (1992), p. 78.

106 *"Truly, the greatest"* Lao Tzu (1992a), p. 96.

107 *"Elvis's life was"* DePaoli, p. 9.

107 *"A big part"* Haining, pp. 161–162.

107 *"Elvis, like America"* DePaoli, p. 17.

107 *"It was strange"* Haining, p. 152.

108 *Transcendence is a step* Rosen (2002), p. xxx.

108 *"Millions of people"* Geller, p. 142.

108 *"So be it"* Ibid., p. 142.

108 *When ten years later* Ibid., p. 232.

108 *"God works in"* Ibid., p. 233.

28: SUCCESS AND FAILURE

109 *"You don't have"* Lao Tzu (1996), p. 18.

110 *"When you are"* Lao Tzu (1992b), p. 117.

110 *"He does not"* Chuang Tzu (1992), p. 130.

110 *"Let those who"* Lao Tzu (1996), p. 46.

110 *"The vanity of"* Ibid., p. 18.

111 *"Elvis would be"* Clayton, p. 90.

111 *"It was not"* DePaoli, p. 96.

111 *"Elvis got assassinated"* Ludwig, p. 169.

111 *"Elvis dug his"* Nash, p. 763.

112 *"Rising from rural"* DePaoli, p. 97.

112 *"success is as"* Lao Tzu (1988), No. 13.

29: HOME (GRACELAND)

113 *"And though of"* Gibran, p. 37.

114 *"The Tao protects"* Lao Tzu (1985), p. 137.

114 *"Tao is the"* Ibid., p. 55.

114 *"Houses full of"* Lao Tzu (1996), p. 18.

114 *"Retreating to hide"* Lü, p. 63.

115 *"I only really"* Farren, p. 99.

115 *"My mama was"* Geller, p. 35.

115 *"I had never"* Guralnick (1994), p. 468.

115 *"It turned out"* Comments made by Mary Pipher in a letter to the author after a visit to Graceland, 1996.

116 *Graceland was more* Guralnick (1999), pp. 222–223.

116 *"No matter what"* Iyer, p. 251.

116 *This spiritual ritual* Durkheim described this kind of *rite of passage* as a religious "collective effervescence, when human beings feel themselves transformed, and are in fact transformed, through ritual doing. A force experienced as external to each individual is the agent of that transformation, but the force itself is created by the fact of assembling

and temporarily living a collective life that transports individuals beyond themselves." Durkheim, p. xli.

30: KING

117 *"The king is"*   Carleton, p. 87.

118 *"Use the Tao"*   Lao Tzu (1996), p. 60.

118 *"The Tao is"*   Ibid., p. 50.

118 *"Kings would fall"*   Ibid., p. 78.

118 *"When you realize"*   Lao Tzu (1988), No. 16.

119 *"I'm not the King"*   Haining, p. 147.

119 *"[Elvis] knew exactly"*   Nash, p. 585.

119 *"When the King"*   Ludwig, p. 143.

119 *"He was, and"*   DePaoli, p. 77.

120 *"I looked into"*   Chuang Tzu (1992), pp. 192–193.

31: PAIN AND SUFFERING

121 *"And you would"*   Gibran, pp. 58–59.

122 *"We ache, because"*   Ming-Dao (1996), p. 95.

122 *"One of the"*   Ibid., p. 168.

122 *"If he gives"*   I Ching (1967), p. 233.

122 *"Clouds and thunder"*   Ibid., p. 17.

123 *"The fans, the"*   Geller, p. 286.

123 *"When you chronicle"*   Nash, p. 141.

123 *"He'd go to"*   Ibid., p. 365.

123 *"Those last five"*   Ibid., p. 531.

124 *"He already seemed"*   Guralnick (1999), p. 603.

32: HARMONY AND BALANCE

125 *"Perfect harmony is"*   Lao Tzu (1996), p. 131.

126 *"The Tao moves"*   Ibid., p. 80.

126 *"All things have"*   Lao Tzu (1985), No. 42, p. 46.

126 *"Those who cultivate"*   Lao Tzu (1996), p. 81.

126 *"Simply balance the"*   Lao Tzu (1992a), p. 56.

127 *"Gospel music became"*   Farren, p. 29.

127 *"Elvis was harangued"*   DePaoli, p. 18.

127 *"He was a real"*   Haining, p. 160.

127 *"If we make"*   Stanley, pp. 203–204.

128 *"He got what"*   Interview with Alfred Wertheimer on National Public Radio (in which he quoted Little Richard), December 1, 1997.

33: PRISONER AND FREEDOM

129 *"The worst"* Ming-Dao (1996), p. 211.

130 *"Care about people's"* Lao Tzu (1988), No. 9.

130 *"Be content with"* Chuang Tzu (1974), p. 59.

130 *"Addiction is most"* Ming-Dao (1996), p. 211.

130 *"He comes very"* I Ching, (1967), p. 184.

131 *"What drove us"* Geller, pp. 23–24.

131 *"I know what"* Ibid., pp. 13–14.

131 *"The spiritual"* Ibid., p. 155.

131 *"Elvis was like"* Clayton, p. 296.

132 *the Comeback Special* This live TV broadcast on NBC in 1968 was orchestrated by Elvis, but opposed by the Colonel. It marked the end of the cookie-cutter movies and the renewal of live performances, which Elvis faithfully executed until his death.

34: DESTINY

133 *"In a real"* Brussat, p. 471.

134 *"Nothing is better"* Chuang Tzu (1994), p. 35.

134 *"Find out destiny"* Lao Tzu (1992b), No. 51, p. 48.

134 *"Their lives appear"* Ming-Dao (1996), pp. 68–69.

134 *"The Master does"* Lao Tzu (1988), No. 30.

135 *"I always felt"* Farren, p. 10.

135 *"Elvis saw Jesse's"* Geller, p. 132.

135 *"I think Elvis"* Clayton, p. 254.

135 *"He was destiny's"* Nash, p. 231.

136 *"The Way is"* Lao Tzu (1992b), No. 61, p. 55.

136 *"No one can"* Ming-Dao (1996), p. 63.

35: MEDITATION AND HEALTH

137 *"How can I"* Griffiths, p. 35.

138 *"When your mind"* Lao Tzu (1992a), p. 14.

138 *"If you want"* Ming-Dao (1996), p. 200.

138 *"To know peace"* Lao Tzu (1985), No. 55, p. 52.

138 *"Those of us"* Ming-Dao (1996), p. 17.

139 *"Elvis really took"* Geller, p. 127.

139 *"Meditation is better"* Ibid., p. 127.

139 *"Many of his"* Ibid., p. 71.

139 *"I asked him"* Clayton, p. 366. Janelle McComb actualized Elvis's wish and saw to it that a memorial chapel was built in Tupelo,

Mississippi, next to the house where he was born. It opened August 19, 1979.

140 *"Gospel singing"* Stanley, p. 20.

140 *"Keep your eyes"* Juanico, pp. 129–130.

36: MADNESS AND ILLNESS

141 *"Which is worse"* Ming-Dao (1996), p. 188.

142 *"Only I am"* Lao Tzu (1985), No. 20, p. 35.

142 *"The brighter it"* Lao Tzu (1996), p. 18.

142 *"Without controlling"* Ming-Dao (1996), p. 102.

142 *"When illness is"* Ibid., p. 179.

143 *"People will come"* Guralnick (1999), p. 411. Told to Kathy Westmoreland (singer who worked with Elvis; she also was his lover and friend) as she and Elvis watched crowds arrive, when on tour in 1970. Kathy noted that the remark made everyone laugh and that Elvis laughed louder than anyone.

143 *"Elvis was never"* Clayton, p. 190.

143 *"On October"* Guralnick (1999), pp. 514–515.

143 *"[After five years"* Clayton, p. 301.

144 *"Blessed are"* Stanley, p. 12.

144 *"He could be"* Geller, p. 56.

144 *Although Elvis's use* Ibid., pp. 149–150.

144 *"In addition"* Ibid., pp. 191–192.

144 *"Do you think"* and *"Sad to say"* Ibid., p. 192.

144 *"a man suffering"* Guralnick (1999), pp. 555–556.

145 *"I'm self-destructive"* Ibid., p. 556.

145 *"A decisive"* Zimmer, p. 231.

145 *"Change yourself"* Ibid.

145 *"like pinning"* Lao Tzu (1992a), p. 8.

37: COMPASSION AND FORGIVENESS

147 *"If you have"* Ming-Dao (1996), p. 128.

148 *"All people love"* Lao Tzu (1996), p. 135.

148 *"I treasure and"* Ibid., p. 134.

148 *"Those who are"* Ming-Dao (1996), p. 133.

148 *"Through compassion"* I Ching (1982), p. 14.

149 *"Elvis really always"* Geller, p. 55.

149 *"In Monroe"* Clayton, p. 282.

149 *"Elvis assumed"* Stanley, p. 23.

149 *"God, forgive"* Nash, p. 717. On his knees, praying, the day before he died. Recorded by Rick Stanley, who was with him.

150 *"We cannot"* Merton, p. 37.

38: MIRROR

151 *"Elvis presents"* Stanley, p. 15.

152 *"The heart"* Chuang Tzu (1992), p. 119.

152 *"He forgets"* Lao Tzu (1996), pp. 70–71.

152 *"Can you wipe"* Ibid., p. 20.

152 *"Our spirit dwells"* Ibid.

153 *"They had to"* Guralnick (1999), p. 467.

153 *"A deeper truth"* Ibid., p. 469.

153 *"We looked"* Ibid., pp. 149–150. Guralnick also notes that Joe Esposito (a member of the Memphis Mafia) told Elvis that Ann-Margret was "a female you"!

153 *"He was like"* Nash, p. 616.

154 *"For now we"* Geller, p. 178.

154 *"He has discovered"* Ruiz, pp. xviii–xix.

154 *"capacity for"* Bosnak, p. 195.

39: PURPOSE AND MEANING

155 *"Tao is everything"* Ming-Dao (1996), p. 201.

156 *"It's important"* Ibid., p. 23.

156 *"When you do"* Ibid., p. 108.

156 *"Other people"* Lao Tzu (1988), No. 20.

156 *"Because he"* Ibid., No. 22.

157 *"I've always"* Geller, p. 33.

157 *"There's a meaning"* Ibid., p. 34.

157 *"All I knew"* Ibid., p. 45.

157 *"For someone"* Ibid., p. 53.

158 *"the culmination"* Whitmer, p. 412.

158 *"Self-purification"* Elvis wrote this passage in the margin of page 195 in *Letters of Helene Roerich* (a photocopy of the page was provided by Larry Geller).

40: PRAYER AND SACRIFICE

159 *"Each one prays"* Official Mahatma Gandhi website http://www.mkgandhi.org

160 *"Prayer is a"* Ming-Dao (1996), p. 158.

160 *"We are moved"* Ibid., p. 158.

160 *"The gods... will"* Ming-Dao (1993), p. 4.

160 *"Heaven and Earth"* Lao Tzu (1985), No. 5, p. 28.

161 *"I cried out"* Geller, p. 110.

161 *"I took both"* Guralnick (1999), p. 617.

161 *"He felt like"* Ibid., p. 636.

161 *"Dear Lord"* Stanley, p. 142.

162 *"The king's way"* Zimmer, p. 232.

41: DEATH AND REBIRTH

163 *"Estranged and re-united"* Chisled in stone at the entrance to the Tillich Garden where Paul Tillich is buried in New Harmony, Indiana.

164 *"Daring to act"* Lao Tzu (1996), p. 146.

164 *"The strong do"* Lao Tzu (1985), No. 42, p. 46.

164 *"Going out is"* Ibid., No. 50, p. 49.

164 *"Who uses his"* Lao Tzu (1996), p. 104.

165 *"Don't forget"* Clayton, p. 340.

165 *"I'm not afraid"* Geller, p. 316.

165 *"The soul's free"* Ibid.

165 *"I'm not surprised"* Clayton, p. 360.

166 *"If you didn't"* Geller, p. 300.

166 *"Don't worry"* Ibid., p. 300.

166 *"Look, Larry"* Ibid., p. 300.

166 *"Don't forget"* Ibid., pp. 301–302.

166 *"I, ah, ah"* Ibid., pp. 186–187.

167 *"Elvis was"* Ibid., p. 315.

167 *"It is as"* Ibid., p. 323.

42: SPIRITUAL WHOLENESS

169 *"Pray to roundness"* Lamb, p. 883.

170 *"One is the beginning"* Lao Tzu (1996), p. 78.

170 *"Tao is"* Ibid., p. 124.

170 *"The kingly"* Chuang Tzu (1992), pp. 106–107.

170 *"The universe"* Lao Tzu (1992a), pp. 9, 17, 57.

171 *"God has a reason"* Stearn, p. 97.

171 *"Our soul, our"* Ibid, pp. 245–246.

171 *"Once I go"* Geller, p. 322.

171 *"As Jennifer was"* Moody, p. 61. Sherry Reed also said, "I'll always love Elvis for what he did for Jennifer."

172 *"to cultivate Tao"* Rousselle, p. 64.

172 *"The Way gave"* Lao Tzu (1990), No. 42, p. 9.

172 *"Our true essential nature"* Rousselle, p. 96.

172 *"It turns in"* Lao Tzu (1985), No. 25, p. 37.

172 *"[He] who dies"* Lao Tzu (1996), p. 66.

BIBLIOGRAPHY

Benner, Joseph S. 1969. *The Impersonal Life.* Marina del Rey, Calif.: De Vorss Publications.

Bosnak, Robert. 1993. *A Little Course in Dreams.* Boston: Shambhala.

Brown, Peter H., and Pat H. Broeske. 1997. *Down at the End of Lonely Street: The Life and Death of Elvis Presley.* New York: Dutton.

Buber, Martin. 1960. Symbolic and Sacramental Existence in Judaism. In Campbell, J., ed., *Spiritual Disciplines,* pp. 168–185.

Brussat, Frederic, and Mary Ann Brussat. 1996. *Spiritual Literacy: Reading the Sacred in Everyday Life.* New York: Scribner.

Cammerloher, Moriz. 1960. The Position of Art in the Psychology of Our Time. In Campbell, J., ed. *Spiritual Disciplines,* pp. 424–447.

Campbell, Joseph., ed. 1954. *Spirit and Nature.* Princeton, N.J.: Princeton University Press.

———. 1960. *Spiritual Disciplines.* Princeton, N.J.: Princeton University Press.

Carleton's Hand-Book of Popular Quotations. 1878. New York: G. W. Carleton.

Chuang Tzu. 1974. *Inner Chapters.* Trans. Gia-Fu Feng and Jane English. New York: Vintage.

———. 1992. Readings from Chuang Tzu. In Thomas Merton, *The Way of Chuang Tzu,* pp. 47–240. Boston and London: Shambhala.

———. 1994. *Wandering on the Way.* Trans. Victor H. Mair. New York: Bantam Books.

Clayton, Rose, and Dick Heard, eds. 1994. *Elvis Up Close: In the Words of Those Who Knew Him Best.* Atlanta: Turner.

DePaoli, Geri, ed. 1994. *Elvis + Marilyn: 2 x Immortal.* New York: Rizzoli.

Dundy, Elaine. 1985. *Elvis and Gladys.* New York: Macmillan.

Durkheim, Emile. 1995. *The Elementary Forms of Religious Life.* Trans. Karen E. Fields. New York: Free Press.

Early, G. 1996. The Emerging South of Civil Rights: Martin Luther King, Jr. and Elvis. Keynote address at Second Annual International Conference on Elvis Presley, August 4–9, University of Mississippi.

Edwards, Tyrone, and Ralph E. Browns. 1960. *The New Dictionary of Thoughts.* New York: Standard Book Co.

Eicher, P. 1993. *The Elvis Sightings.* New York: Avon Books.

Erikson, Erik H. 1982. *The Life Cycle Completed: A Review.* New York: Norton.

Estés, Clarissa Pinkola. 1998. Elvis Presley: *Fáma* and the *Cultus* of the Dying God. In *The Soul of Popular Culture.* Kittelson, M. L., (ed.). Peru, Ill: Open Court. pp. 19–50.

Farren, Mick. 1977. *Elvis in His Own Words.* London: Omnibus Press.

Geller, Larry, and Joel Spector, with Patricia Romanowski. 1989. *If I Can Dream: Elvis' Own Story.* New York: Simon and Schuster.

Gibran, Kahlil. 1961. *The Prophet.* New York: Knopf.

Griffiths, Bede. 1976. *Return to the Center.* Springfield, Ill: Templegate.

Guralnick, Peter. 1994. *Last Train to Memphis: The Rise of Elvis Presley.* Boston: Little, Brown and Company.

——. 1999. *Careless Love: The Unmaking of Elvis Presley.* Boston: Little, Brown and Company.

Haining, Peter., ed. 1987. *Elvis in Private.* New York: St. Martin's Press.

Harvey, A., ed. 1998. *The Essential Mystics: The Soul's Journey into Truth.* Edison, N.J.: Castle Books.

Heiler, Friedrich. 1960. Contemplation in Christian Mysticism. In Campbell, J., ed. *Spiritual Disciplines.* Princeton, N.J.: Princeton University Press. pp. 186–238.

Heschel, Abraham I. 1990. *I Asked for Wonder: A Spiritual Anthology.* ed. Samuel H. Dresner. New York: Crossroad.

Higgins, Patrick. 1994. *Before Elvis There Was Nothing.* New York: Carroll and Graf.

I Ching (Book of Changes). 1967. 3rd ed. Trans. Richard Wilhelm. Princeton, N.J.: Princeton University Press.

I Ching (The Illustrated). 1982. Trans. R. L. Wing. New York: Doubleday.

Iyer, Pico. 1992. *The Lady and the Monk.* New York: Vintage.

Juanico, June. 1997. *Elvis: In the Twilight of Memory.* New York: Arcade.

Jung, C. G., 1954. The Phenomenology of the Spirit in Fairy Tales. In

Campbell, J., ed. *Spirit and Nature*. Princeton, N.J.: Princeton University Press. pp. 3–48.

——. 1966a. 2nd ed. Anima and Animus. In *Two Essays on Analytical Psychology*. Vol. 7, *The Collected Works of C. G. Jung (CW)*. Princeton, N.J.: Princeton University Press. pp. 188–211.

——. 1966b. 2nd ed. The Practical Use of Dream-analysis. In *The Practice of Psychotherapy*. Vol. 16, CW. Princeton, N.J.: Princeton University Press. pp. 139–161.

——. 1968. 2nd ed. The Mother Complex. In *The Archetypes and the Collective Unconscious*. Vol. 9, I. CW. Princeton, N.J.: Princeton University Press. pp. 85–110.

——. 1973. *C. G. Jung Letters*. Vol. 1. eds. G. Adler and A. Jaffe. Princeton, N.J.: Princeton University Press.

Kabat-Zinn, Jon. 1994. *Wherever You Go There You Are*. New York: Hyperion.

Kittleson, Mary Lynn. 1998. *The Soul of Popular Culture*. Peru, Ill.: Open Court.

Lamb, Wally. 1998. *I Know This Much Is True*. New York: Regan Books (HarperCollins).

Lao Tzu. 1970. *Springs of Oriental Wisdom*. New York: Herder Books.

——. 1985. *Tao Te Ching: The Richard Wilhelm Edition*. Trans. H. G. Ostwald. London and New York: Arkana/Penguin.

——. 1988. *Tao Te Ching*. Trans. S. Mitchell. New York: HarperCollins.

——. 1990. *Tao Te Ching: The Classic Book of Integrity and the Way*. Trans. V. A. Mair. New York: Bantam Books.

——. 1992a. *Hua Hu Ching (The Unknown Teachings of Lao Tzu)*. Trans. B. Walker. HarperSan Francisco (a division of HarperCollins).

——. 1992b. *Wen-tzu: Understanding the Mysteries (Further Teachings of Lao Tzu)*. Trans. T. Cleary. Boston: Shambhala.

——. 1996. 2nd ed. *Taoteching*. Trans. Red Pine (Bill Porter). San Francisco: Mercury House.

Lü, Tung-pin. 1991. *The Secret of the Golden Flower*. Trans. Thomas Cleary. New York: HarperSan Francisco (a division of HarperCollins).

Ludwig, L., and Solomon B. T. Church, eds. 1995. *The Gospel of Elvis*. Arlington, Tex.: Summit Publishing Group.

Melville, Herman 1991. Art. In *Selected Poems of Herman Melville*. ed. H. Cohen. New York: Fordham University Press.

Merton, Thomas. 1958. *Thoughts in Solitude*. New York: Farrar, Straus, and Giroux.

Miller, D. 1996. *The Tao of Muhammad Ali*. New York: Warner Books.

Ming-Dao, D. 1993. *Chronicles of Tao: The Secret Life of a Taoist Master*. New York: HarperSanFrancisco.

———. 1996. *Everyday Tao: Living with Balance and Harmony*. New York: HarperSanFrancisco (a division of HarperCollins).

Moody, Raymond A. 1989. *Elvis After Life: Unusual Psychic Experiences Surrounding the Death of a Superstar*. New York: Bantam Books.

Nash, Alanna, with Billy Smith, Marty Lacker, and Lamar Fike. 1995. *Elvis Aaron Presley: Revelations from the Memphis Mafia*. New York: HarperCollins.

O'Donohue, J. 1997. *Anam Cara: Spiritual Wisdom from the Celtic World*. London: Bantam.

Pareles, J. 1998. Elvis Lives? In the *New York Times*. 23 March.

Pearlman, J. 1988. *Elvis for Beginners*. London: Unwin Paperbacks.

Presley, Priscilla Beaulieu, with Sandra Harmon. 1985. *Elvis and Me*. New York: Putnam.

Ritzer, George. 1993. *The McDonaldization of Society*. Newbury Park, Calif.: Pine Forge Press.

Rosen, David H. 1997. *The Tao of Jung: The Way of Integrity*. New York: Penguin.

———. 2002. *Transforming Depression: Healing the Soul Through Creativity*. York Beach, Maine: Nicolas-Hays.

Rosen, David H., and Michael C. Luebbert, eds. 1999. *Evolution of the Psyche*. Westport, Conn.: Praeger.

Rousselle, Erwin. 1960. Spiritual Guidance in Contemporary Taoism. In Campbell, J., ed. *Spiritual Disciplines*. pp. 59–101.

Ruiz, Don Miguel. 1997. *The Four Agreements: A Toltec Wisdom Book*. San Rafael, Calif.: Amber-Allen.

Scherman, Roland. 1991. *Elvis Is Everywhere*. New York: Clarkson Potter Publishers.

Shimano, Eido Tai, ed. 1996. *Endless Vow: The Zen Path of Soen Nakagawa*. Boston: Shambhala.

Stanley, Rick, with Paul Harold. 1992. *Caught in a Trap*. Dallas, Tex.: Word Publishing.

Stearn, Jess, with Larry Geller. 1998. *Elvis' Search for God*. Murfreesboro, Tenn.: Greenleaf Publications.

Stevens, Anthony. 1993. *The Two Million-Year-Old Self*. College Station, Tex.: Texas A & M University Press.

Sumner, J. D. 1987. The Man with the Golden Handshakes. In *Elvis in Private.* Ed. Peter Haining. New York: St. Martin's Press.

Walker, Alice. 1989. *The Temple of My Familiar.* San Diego: Harcourt Brace Jovanovich.

Whitmer, Peter. 1996. *The Inner Elvis: A Psychological Biography of Elvis Aaron Presley.* New York: Hyperion.

Yogananda, Paramahansa. 1998. *Autobiography of a Yogi.* Los Angeles: Self-Realization Fellowship.

Zimmer, Heinrich R. 1956. *The King and the Corpse: Tales of the Soul's Conquest of Evil.* Princeton, N.J.: Princeton University Press.

ACKNOWLEDGMENTS

For assistance and friendship while carrying out research in Memphis, I sincerely thank Bill and Anne Kay Walker. During that time, I interviewed Ann Finch, one of Elvis's friends who had not previously been interviewed; and his dentist and friend Dr. Lester Hofman and his wife, Sterling. I want to thank Mandy Graeber, Stacy Stewart, and Annahita Varahrami, three former students of mine, for research work. I'm indebted to Vernon Chadwick, who invited me to present a paper, "Don't Be Cruel to a Heart That's True: Understanding the King and What Went Wrong," as part of the Second International Conference on Elvis Presley, in 1996, at the University of Mississippi in Oxford. Many of the ideas for this book began to take shape prior to, during, and following that event. My friend Margaret Wilkinson joined me in Oxford and on a subsequent trip to Elvis's birthplace, in Tupelo. I extend warm thanks to her for her encouragement and support of this project over the years. A kind thank you to Mary Pipher, Ph.D. (author of *Reviving Ophelia* and other works), who gave me permission to quote from an unpublished account of her visit to Graceland. Heartfelt thanks to my dear friend and soul sister Clarissa Pinkola Estes, Ph.D. (author of *Women Who Run with the Wolves* and other books), for permission to quote from her eloquent published piece on Elvis, someone she understands and loves. I dearly thank Alice Walker (author of *The Color Purple* and other books) for permission to quote from her comments on Elvis in *The Temple of My Familiar*. I also express my deep gratitude to Larry Geller (Elvis's spiritual adviser and the co-author of *If I Can Dream: Elvis's Own Story*), who shared much about Elvis's spiritual quest, including one of Elvis's religious books containing Elvis's notes in the margins. In addition, I express many thanks to the following readers and critics who helped make this a better book: Valerie Andrews, Kathi Appelt, Paula Bonner, Sharon Broll, Regula Buchi, Tim Hamilton, Toni King, Stipe Mestrovic, Nancy Rosen, Armin Schmidt, Jo Spiller, David Stanford, Lolly Torbet, Diane Walsh, Joel Weishaus, Flor Whittaker, Margaret

Wilkinson, and Miranda Zent. In particular, Stipe Mestrovic, Diane Walsh, and Joel Weishaus offered many excellent ideas and wise suggestions. A special acknowledgment and thank you to Angela Lozano, Annahita Varahrami, and Jillian Somers, who typed early and final versions of the manuscript—Annahita and Jillian did the most, and always with gracious smiles. A huge thanks to my editor at Harcourt, Kati Steele Hesford. She was the perfect midwife for the birth of this book. Celebratory thanks to Erin Gross, editorial assistant, and Gayle Feallock, managing editor. Last but not least, a love-filled thanks to my three daughters, Sarah, Laura, and Rachel. All three endured, mostly with smiles, hearing all about Elvis, and over the years they've listened, and danced, to many of his songs. But it was guitar-playing Rachel who enjoyed Elvis the most, and from the start she was excited about this book. Once she even had me take a Teddy Bear from her fifth-grade class on a tour of Graceland, and we've got photographs to prove it!

PERMISSIONS
ACKNOWLEDGMENTS

We acknowledge use of excerpted material from the following publications:

Chuang Tzu, "The Readings from Chuang Tzu" in *The Way of Chuang Tzu*, translated by Thomas Merton. Copyright © 1965 by the Abbey of Gethsemani. Reprinted with permission of New Directions Publishing Corporation and Laurence Pollinger Limited. Published in Great Britain by Search Press Ltd.

Clayton, Rose and Dick Heard, eds., *Elvis Up Close: In the Words of Those Who Knew Him Best*. Copyright © 1994 by Rose M. Clayton and Richard M. Heard. Reprinted with permission of Rose Clayton.

Geller, Larry and Joel Spector with Patricia Romanowski, *"If I Can Dream": Elvis' Own Story*. Copyright © 1989 by Larry Geller and Joel Spector. Reprinted with permission of Larry Geller.

Gibran, Kahlil, *The Prophet*. Copyright © 1923 by Kahlil Gibran and renewed in 1951 by Administrators C.T.A. of Kahlil Gibran Estate and Mary G. Gibran. Reprinted with permission of Alfred A. Knopf, a division of Random House, Inc. and the Gibran National Committee in Beirut, Lebanon.

Gurlanick, Peter, *Last Train to Memphis*. Copyright © 1994 by Peter Gurlanick. *Careless Love* copyright © 1999 by Peter Guralnick. Reprinted with permission of Little Brown & Company, (Inc.).

Lao Tzu, *Tao Te Ching: The Book of Meaning and Life*, translated by Richard Wilhelm, translated by H. G. Ostwald (Arkana, 1989) copyright © Eugen Diederichs Verlag Gm Bh & Co. Koln, 1985. English translation copyright © Routledge & Kegan Paul, 1985. Reprinted with permission of Penguin Books (UK), Ltd.